HOUSING ISSUES, LAWS AND PROGRAMS

FEDERAL HOUSING ASSISTANCE PROGRAMS FOR LOW-INCOME HOUSEHOLDS

Housing Issues, Laws and Programs

Additional books in this series can be found on Nova's website under the Series tab.

Additional e-books in this series can be found on Nova's website under the e-book tab.

HOUSING ISSUES, LAWS AND PROGRAMS

FEDERAL HOUSING ASSISTANCE PROGRAMS FOR LOW-INCOME HOUSEHOLDS

ERIC COLLIER
EDITOR

nova publishers
New York

Library of Congress Cataloging-in-Publication Data

ISBN: 978-1-63484-336-2

Published by Nova Science Publishers, Inc. † New York

CONTENTS

PREFACE

In 2014, the federal government provided about $50 billion in housing assistance specifically designated for low-income households. That assistance—which is made available both through spending programs and preferential tax treatment—increased by about 15 percent in real (inflation-adjusted) terms between 2000 and 2003. Since that time, such assistance has remained relatively stable at about $50 billion annually (measured in 2014 dollars), with the exception of a temporary boost, mostly in 2010 and 2011, associated with the American Recovery and Reinvestment Act of 2009 (ARRA). The Congressional Budget Office report, provided in this book, discusses the ways in which the federal government provides housing assistance to low-income households, examines how that assistance has changed since 2000, and provides information about the households that receive assistance. In addition, the book assesses policy options for altering that assistance. The book also identifies the federal, state, and local government funded programs that provide rental assistance to low-income households and identifies indications of program fragmentation and overlap; assesses the extent of intergovernmental collaboration for rental assistance; and determines what is known about performance at the federal level, at selected state and local jurisdictions and for the collective performance of the levels of government providing rental assistance.

In: Federal Housing Assistance Programs ... ISBN: 978-1-63484-336-2
Editor: Eric Collier

Chapter 1

FEDERAL HOUSING ASSISTANCE FOR LOW-INCOME HOUSEHOLDS*

Natalie Tawil

SUMMARY

In 2014, the federal government provided about $50 billion in housing assistance specifically designated for low-income households. That assistance—which is made available both through spending programs and preferential tax treatment—increased by about 15 percent in real (inflation-adjusted) terms between 2000 and 2003. Since that time, such assistance has remained relatively stable at about $50 billion annually (measured in 2014 dollars), with the exception of a temporary boost, mostly in 2010 and 2011, associated with the American Recovery and Reinvestment Act of 2009 (ARRA).

Unlike some means-tested programs (such as the Supplemental Nutrition Assistance Program, or SNAP) that are intended to assist all eligible people who apply, means-tested housing assistance has not been made available to all applicants who are eligible. Currently, only about one-quarter of the eligible low-income population receives housing assistance through federal spending programs. Households that receive assistance are generally required to pay 30 percent of their income toward their housing expenses, a threshold widely described as affordable.

* This is an edited, reformatted and augmented version of a report issued by the Congressional Budget Office, September 2015.

This Congressional Budget Office report discusses the ways in which the federal government provides housing assistance to low-income households, examines how that assistance has changed since 2000, and provides information about the households that receive assistance. In addition, the report assesses policy options for altering that assistance. Some options would provide substantial budgetary savings over the 2016–2025 period considered in CBO's analysis and others would involve substantial costs.

WHAT HOUSING ASSISTANCE DOES THE FEDERAL GOVERNMENT PROVIDE?

Three spending programs account for the majority of the assistance provided directly to low-income households:

- The Housing Choice Voucher (HCV) program—with $18 billion in spending in 2014—provides federally funded, portable vouchers that recipients use to help pay for housing they choose in the private market.
- Project-based rental assistance (PBRA)—with $12 billion in spending in 2014—provides for federally contracted and subsidized rent in designated buildings that are privately owned and operated.
- Public housing—at a cost of $7 billion in 2014— provides for federally subsidized rent in buildings that are publicly owned and operated.

In addition, the federal government provided about $8 billion in 2014 for other housing programs. Most of that was in the form of grants to state and local governments.

One tax credit, the Low-Income Housing Tax Credit (LIHTC), accounts for most of the assistance provided indirectly to low-income households. It is available to developers of low-income housing and, according to an estimate by the staff of the Joint Committee on Taxation (JCT), accounted for $7 billion in tax expenditures in 2014. Tax expenditures resemble government spending programs in that they provide financial assistance to specific entities or groups of people or for designated activities.

The federal government provided much more support through the tax code, about $130 billion in 2014, for housing not targeted at low-income households—mostly through the tax deductions for mortgage interest payments and for property taxes. Although beyond the scope of this report, that and other types of assistance not focused on low-income households are described in the appendix.

HOW HAS FEDERAL ASSISTANCE FOR LOW-INCOME HOUSING CHANGED?

In 2014, federal housing assistance for low-income households was 15 percent greater in real terms than in 2000. Most of that growth had occurred by 2003. Since then, support has consistently been about $50 billion annually (in 2014 dollars), although federal assistance was temporarily higher, mainly in 2010 and 2011, because of funds provided through ARRA. ARRA spending aside, discretionary spending on federal housing assistance declined in real terms by about 6 percent between 2011 and 2014. (Discretionary spending is decided upon annually by lawmakers in the appropriation process and constitutes about 90 percent of federal support for low-income housing.) That decline followed enactment of the Budget Control Act of 2011, which capped total nondefense discretionary spending.

Over time, the composition of federal assistance has changed as lawmakers have relied more on the private sector to provide low-income housing. Since 2000, measured in real terms, spending on the voucher program and project-based assistance has grown by about one-third, spending on public housing has declined by the same fraction, and tax expenditures for the LIHTC have increased.

WHOM DO FEDERAL LOW-INCOME HOUSING PROGRAMS ASSIST?

The federal government's three main spending programs for low-income housing provide assistance to 4.8 million low-income households.[1] Initial eligibility for federal housing programs is limited to households with no more than 50 percent of area median income (AMI), and roughly three-quarters of the assisted households have income of no more than 30 percent of AMI. The households that receive assistance comprise 9.8 million people, or roughly 3 percent of the U.S. population.

Of those households, almost one-half are headed by people who are neither elderly (defined by the Department of Housing and Urban Development as age 62 or older) nor disabled—yet work is the largest source of income for only about half of households headed by such people.

Housing assistance, like many programs that provide support to low-income populations, provides some incentives that may support employment and others that may discourage employment. Recent studies find that the assistance reduces employment by about 5 percent and earnings (an indicator of hours worked) by about 10 percent.

Households that receive assistance are generally required to pay 30 percent of their income toward their housing expenses. In contrast, of the eligible population that does not receive housing assistance—roughly 14 million households—about six out of seven pay more than 30 percent of their income toward housing expenses. Well over half pay more than 50 percent of their income in rent.

How Could Policymakers Change Federal Low-Income Housing Assistance?

With the federal government facing ongoing fiscal challenges and families facing ongoing economic challenges, the Congress may wish to consider options to restructure programs and tax policies that provide housing assistance for low-income households. This report considers four sets of such options. Most of the options affect discretionary spending—the part of the federal budget that lawmakers control through annual appropriation acts. To achieve the budgetary effects estimated for those options, lawmakers would need to enact changes to housing laws and adjust appropriations accordingly. Two options affect tax credits: Lawmakers could achieve budgetary effects for those options solely by enacting the changes to tax law. (Estimates of budgetary effects of all options are expressed in nominal dollars and encompass the 10-year period from 2016 through 2025.)

The options that CBO considered include the following:

- Changing the size or composition of the assisted population.
  - Reducing the number of HCVs by 10 percent starting in 2016 would save $18 billion over the next 10 years, and gradually eliminating all HCVs would save $118 billion, CBO estimates. Increasing the number of HCVs by 10 percent would cost $18

billion, and offering assistance to all of the currently eligible population would cost $410 billion.
    - Requiring tenants who are neither elderly nor disabled to work toward leaving assisted housing by participating in a self-sufficiency program would cost roughly $10 billion if the number of assisted households was held constant.
- Modifying tenants' contributions to rent.
    - Increasing or decreasing the share of income that tenants contributed toward rent by 5 percentage points would save or cost $22 billion over the 10-year period, by CBO's estimates. Savings would result if tenants were required to pay 35 percent of their income toward rent; costs would result if tenants were required to pay 25 percent of their income toward rent.
- Changing the resources available to the local public housing agencies (PHAs) that administer the programs.
    - Enhancing the ability of PHAs to borrow money from private sources—for example, by allowing them to commit future appropriations to repay those loans—could enable them to obtain capital for the improvement of public housing properties sooner. This option would not affect the federal budget, but whether funds would be forthcoming would depend on the private sector's willingness to make such loans.
    - Requiring the consolidation of PHAs to lower the costs of performing administrative tasks and decreasing funding for the administration of housing assistance could reduce federal spending. CBO does not have sufficient information to estimate the associated effect on the budget.
    - Fully funding PHAs' administrative responsibilities according to the formula amounts outlined in appropriation acts and federal regulations would cost $4 billion over the 10-year period compared with maintaining funding in real terms at the 2014 level, CBO estimates.
- Changing the ways in which housing assistance is provided.
    - Replacing PBRA contracts with HCVs might produce budgetary savings, but CBO does not have sufficient information to estimate the associated effect on the budget.
- Providing money for the Housing Trust Fund established by the Housing and Economic Recovery Act of 2008 would lead to an

increase in federal spending commensurate with the decision made by lawmakers.

- Repealing the LIHTC would increase revenues by $42 billion from 2016 to 2025, according to an estimate by JCT.
- Introducing a renter's tax credit for low-income households, designed to cost the same as the LIHTC, would reduce revenues by $42 billion from 2016 to 2025.

FEDERAL HOUSING ASSISTANCE PROGRAMS FOR LOW-INCOME HOUSEHOLDS

In 2014 the federal government provided $51 billion in low-income housing assistance. Three spending programs—the Housing Choice Voucher program, project-based rental assistance, and public housing—together accounted for $36 billion. The federal government also supplied $7 billion in assistance for low-income tenants through the Low-Income Housing Tax Credit.[2] Several other programs together provided an additional $8 billion for federal housing assistance for low-income households, primarily through grants, most of which went to state and local governments. By comparison, the federal government provided much more support for housing that does not depend on the income of the household. That support, which amounted to about $130 billion in 2014, mostly takes the form of preferential tax treatment—that is, tax expenditures—for homeowners.[3] The tax deduction for mortgage interest payments on owner-occupied residences accounts for most of those tax expenditures and accrues mostly to tax filers in the highest income quintile (See the appendix).

Housing Choice Vouchers

The Housing Choice Voucher program accounted for $18 billion in federal spending in 2014. Vouchers help tenants pay the rent for housing of their choice.[4] Assisted households pay a portion of their income for rent on units they find in the private housing market—as long as property owners agree to participate in the program— and the vouchers cover the balance of their rent up to limits established by the Department of Housing and Urban Development (HUD).[5] Tenants' rental payments are usually 30 percent of their adjusted household income—gross income less deductions, such as those for dependents and for certain medical and child care expenses. The value of the voucher is the difference between the household's rental payment and the limit on rent, which is typically between 90 percent and 110 percent of fair market rents (FMRs) in the area. The limits on rent are determined each fiscal year by HUD on the basis of area rents charged for standard rental housing. Depending on the area, HUD sets the FMRs (which also include the cost of all tenant-paid utilities, except for telephone, television, and Internet service) so that either 40 percent or 50 percent of area rents fall below it. Tenants can continue to use their vouchers when they change residences.

Project-Based Rental Assistance

Project-based rental assistance accounted for $12 billion in federal spending in 2014. Assisted tenants usually pay 30 percent of their adjusted household income toward rent in designated buildings. The federal government pays the balance of the rent, sometimes according to long-term contracts entered into with property owners who agree to provide the low-income housing. Over 30 years ago, lawmakers repealed the authority to use PBRA funds for new construction or the substantial rehabilitation of housing units generally; however, properties specifically designated for the elderly or the disabled can still be funded.[6] Expiring PBRA contracts may be renewed on an annual or multiyear basis, but payments are subject to annual appropriations.[7]

Public Housing

Public housing accounted for $7 billion in federal spending in 2014. Assisted tenants usually pay 30 percent of their adjusted household income toward rent for units that are publicly owned and operated, typically by a local public housing agency (see Box 1).[8] Public housing is supported through two funds, an operating fund and a capital fund; resources for both funds come from annual appropriations. In 2014, lawmakers provided $4.3 billion for the Public Housing Operating Fund and $2.2 billion for the Public Housing Capital Fund. The operating funds are distributed according to a formula that considers PHAs' costs, including the costs of administration and maintenance. Capital spending includes spending on the development, financing, and modernization of public housing. Generally, however, lawmakers have not appropriated funding for public housing development in the past 20 years; and the development of new public housing units had already slowed significantly during the previous decade in favor of providing assistance through the HCV and PBRA programs.

Low-Income Housing Tax Credit

The Low-Income Housing Tax Credit gave rise to $7 billion in tax expenditures in 2014, according to an estimate by JCT. Tax expenditures resemble government spending programs by providing financial assistance to specific activities, entities, or groups of people. For the LIHTC, the federal government allocates a fixed amount of tax credits to the states on the basis of the number of residents (subject to a per-state minimum). States then distribute the credits on a competitive basis to eligible private developers who construct new housing or substantially rehabilitate existing housing and reserve some of the units for low-income households.[9] Developers typically sell the credits to investors to raise capital. Those investors can use the credit to lower their federal tax liability over a period of 10 years.

The LIHTC has been used for more than 40,000 construction projects, and those projects provide almost 90 percent of their units to qualifying low-income households.[10] Tenants of an LIHTC unit reserved for a low-income household pay rent equal to 30 percent of a set portion of the area median income. That portion, either 50 percent or 60 percent of AMI, depends on decisions that the property owner makes about how many units will be reserved for low-income housing and who will be eligible.[11] Surveys have found that about 40 percent of households in units subsidized by the LIHTC also receive some form of direct housing assistance; in those cases, the rent can be determined by the direct assistance program and the tenant contributes 30 percent of household income toward rent.[12] (Federal law requires owners of properties that benefit from the LIHTC to accept vouchers, and owners can enter into project-based rental assistance contracts for properties that benefit from the LIHTC.)

Box 1. The Role of Public Housing Agencies

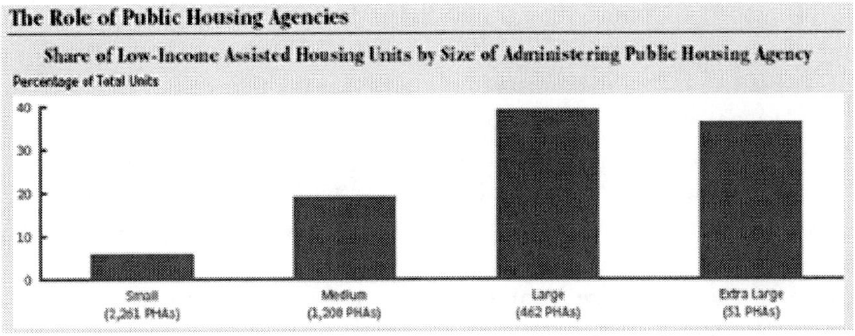

Source: Congressional Budget Office based on data from the Department of Housing and Urban Development, "Public Housing Agency (PHA) Inventory" (updated March 15, 2015), http://go.usa.gov/3F58w. The most recent available data are current as of December 19, 2012.

Note: A small public housing agency administers fewer than 250 units. A medium-sized PHA administers between 250 units and 1,249 units. A large PHA administers between 1,250 units and 9,999 units. An extra-large PHA administers 10,000 units or more.

Total units encompass the Housing Choice Voucher program, project-based rental assistance, and public housing.

Federal housing assistance provided directly to low-income tenants is administered in part by local public housing agencies (PHAs) established by, and operating subject to, state law. PHAs own and operate public housing units, issue housing choice vouchers (HCVs), and in some cases administer project-based rental assistance (PBRA). The jurisdictions of the country's nearly 4,000 PHAs vary widely. Some are regional, as are housing markets, but others cover a city, a county, or only part of a city or county. The number and organization of PHAs within each state reflect the various state policy objectives and different municipal and county governance structures in place when lawmakers first allocated funds for states to establish PHAs through the U.S. Housing Act of 1937. When lawmakers later introduced housing vouchers, the criteria for distributing funds encouraged states to create additional PHAs.

The number of housing units that PHAs administer varies greatly. The New York City Housing Authority is the country's largest PHA and administers nearly 300,000 units. In contrast, there are 64 PHAs in the Greater Boston area, and 34 of those administer fewer than 250 housing units.[1]

Large PHAs are responsible for most of the units receiving direct assistance from the federal government, but the majority of PHAs are small.

Together, the more than 2,000 PHAs that administer fewer than 250 units each are responsible for only 6 percent of all the units in the combined HCV, PBRA, and public housing programs (see the figure).

PHA operations receive federal funds through a few different avenues. Amounts appropriated for the Public Housing Operating Fund are distributed to PHAs on the basis of a formula that takes into account the characteristics of the projects they administer. Amounts provided for administering the HCV program are based on a formula that takes into account the number of units under lease that are administered by the PHA, the fair market rent of a typical unit in the early 1990s, and an indicator of changes in administrative costs over time.[2] Amounts appropriated for the administration of PBRA are small because PHAs are not responsible for most PBRA contracts.

[1] See Department of Housing and Urban Development, "Public Housing Agency (PHA) Inventory" (updated March 15, 2015), http://go.usa.gov/3F58w. The most recent available data are current as of December 19, 2012.

[2] For each unit administered, the formula provides for roughly 7.5 percent of the higher of the FMR for a two-bedroom unit in 1993 or 1994, with all PHAs receiving comparable per-unit rates up to a certain number of units and a slightly lower per-unit rate applied beyond that number. The per-unit rates are adjusted annually using local data about wage rates. See Department of Housing and Urban Development, Office of Public and Indian Housing, "Streamlining Administrative Practices in the Housing Choice Voucher Program," Notice PIH 2012-15 (HA) (February 27, 2012), http://go.usa.gov/3F5EB (PDF, 117 KB); and Section 8(q)(1) of the Housing Act of 1937 (codified at 42 U.S.C. §1437f(q)(1) (2012)).

Other Housing Programs

Other smaller housing assistance programs accounted for $8 billion in federal spending and tax expenditures in 2014. About half of the spending, which was provided primarily through grants to state and local governments, supported programs that provide assistance to designated populations, including homeless people and rural residents. Roughly one-third of the spending was associated with the Community Development Block Grant (CDBG) program and the HOME Investment Partnerships Program. (As part of the CDBG program's mandate to support community and economic development efforts, it can provide funds to low-income households to support homeownership; recipients can also use CDBG funds to acquire property for low-income rental housing or to rehabilitate such housing. And the HOME Investment Partnerships Program helps people in low-income households buy and renovate homes, and provides other kinds of support.) Additional support, about one-tenth of the total, took the form of tax expenditures for private activity bonds for rental housing in which a specified percentage of the units are reserved for low-income households.[13]

Starting in 2015, Fannie Mae and Freddie Mac are required to allocate an amount equal to a specified percentage of their new mortgage purchases to fund the Housing Trust Fund—which will provide formula grants to state and local governments for the production or preservation of low-income housing.[14] Operation of the trust fund, which was originally authorized by the Housing and Economic Recovery Act of 2008, was delayed when the Federal Housing Finance Agency suspended the allocations by Fannie Mae and Freddie Mac because of their financial difficulties stemming from the housing and foreclosure crisis.

However, the agency reinstated the allocations effective in January 2015.[15]

Changes in Federal Support for Low-Income Housing

Total federal housing assistance for low-income households was 15 percent greater in 2014 than in 2000, after adjusting for the effects of inflation (see Figure 1). Almost all of that growth occurred between 2000 and 2003. Since 2003, total support has been about $50 billion annually (measured in 2014 dollars)—although it was temporarily higher, mainly in 2010 and 2011, because of funds provided by ARRA (see Box 2). In 2011, total federal support reached a high of about $60 billion (in 2014 dollars).

The Budget Control Act of 2011 established annual caps on total discretionary appropriations for nondefense programs, although not for individual programs. In 2011 housing assistance for low-income households—which is provided largely through discretionary spending— accounted for 7 percent of nondefense discretionary spending. In 2014, such assistance still accounted for 7 percent of nondefense discretionary spending; however, after the temporary boost to spending that resulted from ARRA is subtracted, discretionary spending on housing assistance for low-income households was 6 percent less (in real terms) in 2014 than in 2011.

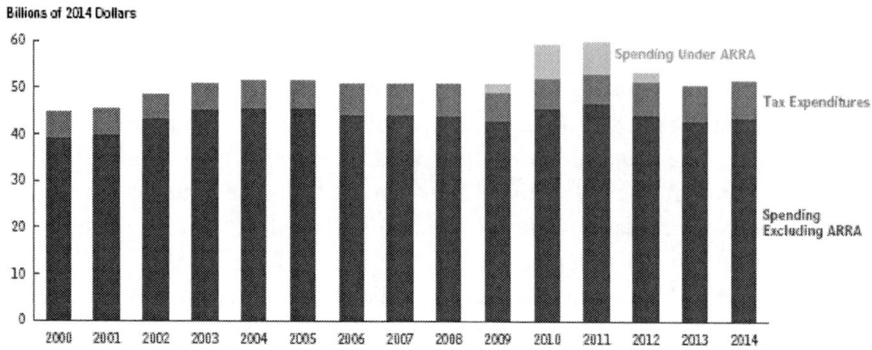

Source: Congressional Budget Office based on data from the Office of Management and Budget, Budget of the U.S. Government, Fiscal Year 2016: Supplemental Materials, "Public Budget Database—Outlays" (February 2015), www.whitehouse.gov/omb/budget/ supplemental, and the staff of the Joint Committee on Taxation, Estimates of Federal Tax Expenditures: Fiscal Year (various years), www.jct.gov/publications.html?func=select&id=5.

Notes: Estimates of federal spending and tax expenditures for low-income housing assistance are expressed in real (inflation-adjusted) dollars. Values are adjusted for inflation using the gross domestic product price index.

Tax expenditures resemble government spending programs in that they provide financial assistance to specific entities or groups of people or for designated activities. The estimates of tax expenditures do not take into account interactions between individual provisions.

ARRA = American Recovery and Reinvestment Act of 2009.

Figure 1. Federal Spending and Tax Expenditures for Low-Income Housing Assistance, 2000 to 2014.

Despite the decline in real terms in spending for housing assistance, HUD and PHAs have taken actions to maintain the number of households receiving assistance, but those actions are not necessarily sustainable (see Box 3).

Box 2. Spending for Federal Housing Assistance for Low-Income Households Under the American Recovery and Reinvestment Act of 2009

Under the American Recovery and Reinvestment Act of 2009 (ARRA), spending for housing assistance programs amounted to $17.2 billion (in 2014 dollars). More than one-third of that amount went to projects that had received assistance from the Low-Income Housing Tax Credit (LIHTC).

Public housing improvements accounted for about one-quarter of that spending, as did the combination of community development programs and assistance to the homeless. The rest went to owners of project-based rental assistance (PBRA) properties. (The amounts presented below are expressed in 2014 dollars.)

The Tax Credit Assistance Program, created by ARRA, provided $6.0 billion in grants for LIHTC projects. The grants were designed to provide financing for developers that had received tax credits between the third quarters of 2006 and 2009. Those tax credits did not have the intended effect because demand for LIHTCs fell with the economic downturn that began in late 2007 and the collapse of the housing market. The most significant LIHTC investors—large banks, Fannie Mae, and Freddie Mac—incurred substantial losses and therefore had little use for tax credits.[1]

ARRA also provided $4.2 billion to the public housing program for capital activities (such as financing and modernization) and management activities. Most of that total was allocated in proportion to previous capital funding for public housing, but one-quarter, or about $1 billion, was distributed on a competitive basis and reserved for priority investments, such as those that leveraged private-sector funds or that financed renovations and energy conservation retrofits. Additionally, ARRA provided $4.7 billion for community development programs that provide low-income housing and for programs that offer assistance to the homeless, including $2.4 billion for the HOME Investment Partnerships Program, $1.6 billion for homelessness prevention and rapid rehousing, $0.5 billion for the Native American Housing Block Grant program, and $0.3 billion for low-income housing support made available through the Community Development Block Grant program.

Finally, ARRA provided $2.4 billion for the owners of properties receiving project-based rental assistance. Of that amount, $2.1 billion went toward renewing existing contracts on a traditional 12-month cycle rather than the shorter cycles that the Department of Housing and Urban Development had been using to maintain support for those contracts. The remainder was directed toward grants or loans for investments designed to reduce energy costs, reduce water use, improve indoor environmental quality, or provide other environmental benefits.

[1] ARRA also established a budget-neutral program allowing for the exchange of unused LIHTCs that had been awarded for new construction. The "Section 1602" program allowed states to exchange their unused 2008 tax credits and 40 percent of their 2009 tax credits for grants of 85 cents on the dollar.

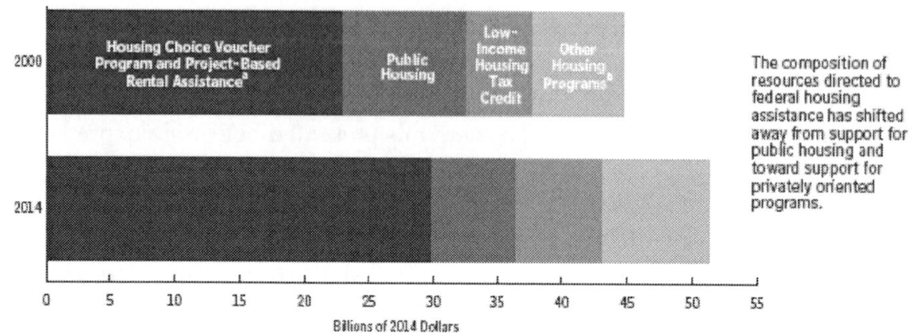

Source: Congressional Budget Office based on data from Office of Management and Budget, Budget of the U.S. Government, Fiscal Year 2016: Supplemental Materials, "Public Budget Database—Outlays" (February 2015), www.whitehouse.gov/omb/budget/supplemental, and the staff of the Joint Committee on Taxation, Estimates of Federal Tax Expenditures: Fiscal Year (various years), www.jct.gov/ publications.html?func=select&id=5.

Note: Estimates of federal spending and tax expenditures for low-income housing assistance are expressed in real (inflation-adjusted) dollars. Values are adjusted for inflation using the gross domestic product price index.

[a] Before 2005, the Housing Choice Voucher program and project-based rental assistance were accounted for jointly in the federal budget as "Rental Assistance."

The category "Other Housing Programs" includes spending targeted by type of recipient (Homeless Assistance, Native American and Hawaiian Assistance, Housing Opportunities for Persons With AIDS, Section 521 and Section 515 assistance for rural rental housing, and Section 502 and Section 504 assistance for rural housing) and spending targeted on the basis of the issue being addressed (HOME Investment Partnerships and Community Development Block Grant support for low-income households—not including spending for disaster recovery). In addition, the category includes tax expenditures for private activity bonds for rental housing in which a percentage of the units are reserved for low-income households. That category does not include spending for Housing Counseling Assistance (to provide any individual or family with advice on seeking, financing, maintaining, renting, or owning a home) or for the Congregate Housing Services Program (which offers grants to provide meals and other supportive services to elderly or disabled residents in federally subsidized housing).

Figure 2. Federal Spending and Tax Expenditures for Low-Income Housing Assistance by Program, 2000 and 2014.

As a result of legislation enacted in the mid-1970s, the composition of resources directed to federal housing assistance began to shift away from support for public housing and toward support for privately oriented programs—HCV, PBRA, and the LIHTC. That trend has continued in recent years (see Figure 2). Over the 2000– 2014 period, real spending for public housing declined by about one-third, or $3.0 billion. During that same period, real spending for HCVs and PBRA increased by about one-third, or $6.9 billion. In addition, since 2000, tax expenditures for the LIHTC have increased by $1.7 billion (in real terms). As a result of those changes in spending, the private sector undertakes more of the building, ownership, and operation of low-income housing. The change in the composition of spending has also reduced the geographic concentration of low-income households and given tenants a greater range of housing options from which to choose.

The decline in real spending for public housing and the increase in resources for the privately oriented programs reflect both legislative choices and economic influences. In terms of legislative choices, lawmakers regularly appropriated funds to provide additional housing choice vouchers, such as those specially designed to assist certain populations (veterans, for instance). Growth in tax expenditures for the LIHTC also reflects actions by lawmakers to expand that program. In addition, lawmakers did not initially index for inflation the LIHTC's population-based state allocations (or the alternative state minimum allocations) but began to do so in 2004.[16] In terms of economic influences, the real cost of providing a given number of vouchers through the HCV program rises when rents increase and income-based rental contributions from tenants fall. In 2010, for example, the inflation-adjusted median monthly rent was 11 percent higher than its 2000 level, and renters' inflation-adjusted median income was 12 percent lower (see Figure 3). Lawmakers have typically provided enough funding to support all previously existing vouchers.

Box 3. Spending for Federal Housing Assistance for Low-Income Households Since Enactment of the Budget Control Act of 2011

The Budget Control Act of 2011, as amended by subsequent legislation, established annual caps through 2021 on total discretionary appropriations for nondefense programs, although it did not specify caps on appropriations for individual programs. Typically, discretionary spending accounts for about 90 percent of federal support for housing assistance for low-income households, and in 2011 that spending amounted to about 7 percent of total nondefense discretionary spending. Discretionary spending on federal housing assistance for low-income households declined by 14 percent in real (inflation-adjusted) terms, from $50.5 billion to $43.6 billion (in 2014 dollars), between 2011 and 2014.

Number of Households That Benefited From Housing Choice Vouchers, Project-Based Rental Assistance, or Public Housing, 2011 to 2014

Millions				
	Housing Choice	Project-Based Rental		
Fiscal Year	Vouchers	Assistancea	Public Housing	Total
2011	2.18	1.52	1.08	4.79
2012	2.21	1.51	1.09	4.81
2013	2.19	1.51	1.09	4.79
2014	2.18	1.50	1.08	4.76

Source: Congressional Budget Office based on data from the Department of Housing and Urban Development, *Annual Performance Plan Fiscal Years 2012–2013* (February 2012), p. 29, http://go.usa.gov/3MqWT (PDF, 1.90 MB); Department of Housing and Urban Development, *FY 2013 Annual Performance Report and FY 2015 Annual Performance Plan* (July 2014), p. 37, http://go.usa.gov/3F5uw; and Todd M. Richardson, Department of Housing and Urban Development, Office of Policy Development and Research, personal communications (January 22, 2015, and March 6, 2015).

Note: This table reflects most of the discretionary spending on housing assistance for low-income households—about 85 percent in 2014, for example—but lawmakers also provide for such spending through Community Development Block Grants, the Department of Agriculture (rural housing), Home Investment Partnerships, Homeless Assistance, Housing Opportunities for Persons With AIDS, and Native American and Hawaiian Assistance.

[a] Households receiving project-based rental assistance include those benefiting from housing for the disabled (Section 811) and housing for the elderly (Section 202).

However, much of that decline was attributable to the end of temporary increases in spending associated with the American Recovery and Reinvestment Act of 2009 (ARRA). Not including ARRA spending, discretionary spending on federal housing assistance for low-income households fell by 6 percent over the 2011–2014 period, from $46.6 billion to $43.6 billion (in 2014 dollars).

Despite that decline in discretionary spending in real terms, the number of assisted households changed little over the period (see the table). That outcome reflects actions taken by the Department of Housing and Urban Development (HUD) and by public housing agencies (PHAs), but those actions are not necessarily sustainable over a longer period.

CBO did not determine which actions were most important in preventing a decline in the number of assisted households. Actions by HUD included signing leases for project-based rental assistance contracts that were in effect for less than 12 months. Such contracts allowed HUD to support, at least temporarily, more households than would have been possible if a larger share of contracts were for a full 12 months. HUD has requested an additional $1 billion in funding for fiscal year 2016 to return to contracts of 12-month duration.[1] HUD also prioritized improvement in occupancy rates of subsidized units. After 2011, the occupancy rate in public housing increased by 1 percentage point (to 96 percent), and the occupancy rate for units under PBRA increased by almost half a percentage point (to 95.2 percent).[2]

PHAs also took steps to avoid a decline in the number of assisted households. For example, in some cases PHAs used their accumulated reserves—subsidy funds received in excess of program expenses in previous years—to finance continued support for assisted households. In some cases, PHAs reduced the maximum amount of rental assistance provided through housing choice vouchers.[3] The value of the voucher is generally between 90 percent and 110 percent of the fair market rent (established by HUD) for an appropriate unit. A PHA may, with HUD's approval, base the value of the voucher on a percentage of fair market rent outside of that 90 percent to 110 percent range. Reductions in the value of the voucher mean that a given amount of federal funds can subsidize more units—but they imply an increase in the assisted household's contribution toward rent, unless the tenants can find and move to a less expensive unit.

[1] See Department of Housing and Urban Development, Congressional Justifications: FY 2016 (February 2015), p. 23-1, http://go.usa.gov/3KwsV.

[2] See Department of Housing and Urban Development, FY2013 Annual Performance Report and FY 2015 Annual Performance Plan (July 2014), pp. 10 and 35, http://go.usa.gov/3F5uw (PDF, 2.35 MB).

[3] See testimony of John Rhea, Chairman, and Cecil House, General Manager, New York City Housing Authority, before the Public Housing and Finance Committees of the New York City Council, *Oversight—Proposed NYCHA Actions to Address the Impact of Federal Sequestration* (June 13, 2013), http://go.usa.gov/3FNWT (PDF, 155 KB).

ELIGIBLE HOUSEHOLDS AND FEDERAL ASSISTANCE

Federal housing assistance for low-income tenants serves about one-quarter of the roughly 20 million households that are eligible. Unlike the means-tested federal support provided to people through programs such as SNAP (formerly known as the Food Stamp program)—which are intended to assist all eligible individuals with specific amounts of income or assets who apply—means-tested housing assistance has not been made available to all applicants who are eligible.

Federal programs are not designed to direct the limited amount of housing assistance exclusively to the lowest-income households; however, federal rules require that a specified minimum percentage of the newly assisted households in the HCV, PBRA, and public housing programs have income of 30 percent of area median income or below (see Table 1). Local public housing authorities may establish their own additional selection requirements.

Households That Receive Federal Assistance

About 5 million households receive federal housing assistance directly through the HCV program, PBRA, or public housing. Those households consist of 9.8 million people, or roughly 3 percent of the U.S. population. The income limit used to determine initial program eligibility is typically no more than 50 percent of AMI. Most of the households receiving assistance have income of no more than 30 percent of AMI, a benchmark that ranged between $7,800 and $36,600 for a family of four in 2013, depending on the area.[17] (By comparison, the federal poverty guideline—commonly referred to as the federal poverty level, or FPL—was $23,550 for a family of four in 2013. The FPL is used in determining financial eligibility for several assistance programs unrelated to housing.)[18]

The average subsidy received by those households in 2013 was $7,600. Gross income per household averaged roughly 25 percent of AMI across the three programs: It averaged about $13,800 in the public housing program, about $13,100 in the HCV program, and about $12,000 in the PBRA program. In PBRA, which has the lowest average household income, half of the households are headed by people who are elderly and close to 20 percent by those who are disabled (see Table 2). Correspondingly, nearly 70 percent of the households receiving PBRA get the largest part of their income from sources that support people who are less likely to be able to work because of age or disability. Those sources include pensions, Social Security, and Supplemental Security Income (SSI), which provides cash assistance to people who are disabled, elderly, or both and who have low income and few assets.

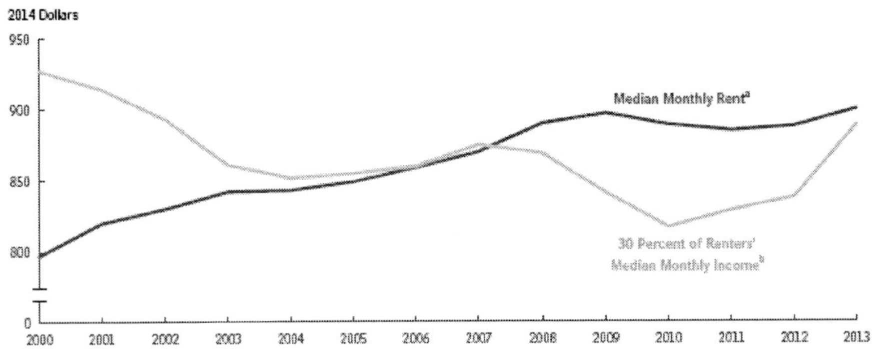

Source: Congressional Budget Office based on calendar year data from the Census Bureau's Current Population Survey, Annual Social and Economic Supplement, and American Housing Survey; and on data from the Bureau of Labor Statistics.

Note: Values are adjusted for inflation using the gross domestic product price index.

[a] Median monthly rent excludes the portion covered by assistance programs and includes utilities. It does not include rents of lodgers (members of households who pay rent to another household member) or of households that pay no rent.

[b] Tenants receiving assistance directly from the federal government typically contribute 30 percent of their household income toward rent. Renters' median monthly income does not include the income of people renting in group quarters (such as dormitories or nursing homes) or of households that pay no rent.

Figure 3. Median Monthly Rent and Income for All Renters, Calendar Years 2000 to 2013.

In contrast, about half of the households served by HCVs and by public housing are headed by people of working age who are able-bodied. Of those households headed by working-age, able-bodied people, only about one-half receive the largest portion of their income from work. The remainder consist of households for which the largest source of income is Temporary Assistance for Needy Families (TANF) and state-funded cash assistance (representing about one-quarter of the households); households for which the largest portion of income comes from other sources, such as child support (representing about one-fifth of the households); and households for which the largest source of income comes from pensions, Social Security, and SSI.

Table 1. Eligibility Rules and Outcomes for Federal Low-Income Housing Assistance

Program	Eligibility for Newly Assisted Households (Based on the Relationship Between Gross Household Income and Area Median Income, or AMI)	Percentage of Newly Assisted Households That Must Have Gross Income of 30 Percent of AMI or Below	Percentage of Assisted Households That Had Gross Income of 30 Percent of AMI or Below in 2013
	Assistance Provided Directly to Tenants		
HCV	50 percent of AMI or below[a]	75	76
PBRA	50 percent of AMI or below[b]	40	75
Public Housing	80 percent of AMI or below	40	72
	Assistance Provided Indirectly to Tenants Through Property Owners		
	Property owner chooses between: 50 percent of AMI or below and		
LIHTC	60 percent of AMI or below[c]	0	40

Source: Congressional Budget Office based on the Department of Housing and Urban Development, Housing Choice Voucher Program Guidebook (April 2001), Chapters 4 and 5, http://go.usa.gov/3ZZr3; Section 8 Project-Based Assistance Programs: Admission, 24 C.F.R. §5.653; Department of Housing and Urban Development, Public Housing Occupancy Guidebook (June 2003), pp. 23 and 34, http://go.usa.gov/3ZZNk; Internal Revenue Code 26 U.S.C. §42(g)(1) (2010); Lynn Rodgers, Department of Housing and Urban Development, personal communication (August 6, 2014); Katherine M. O'Regan and Keren M. Horn, "What Can We Learn About the Low Income Housing Tax Credit Program by Looking at the Tenants?" Housing Policy Debate, vol. 23, no. 3 (May 2013), pp. 597–613, http://dx.doi.org/10.1080/10511482.2013.772909.

Note: HCV = housing choice voucher; LIHTC = Low-Income Housing Tax Credit; PBRA = project-based rental assistance.

[a]Households with gross income of 80 percent of AMI or less are eligible if they have been receiving continued support since entering an assistance program at 50 percent of AMI or less or if they have been displaced as a result of the prepayment of a mortgage or voluntary termination of a mortgage insurance contract.

[b] A limited number of units can be rented to households with gross income of 80 percent of AMI or less.

[c] The applicable payment calculation depends on choices made by the property owner in qualifying for the tax credit.

Table 2. Characteristics of Households Receiving Housing Choice Vouchers, Project-Based Rental Assistance, or Public Housing Assistance, 2013

		Demographics by Household Type					Households' Largest Source of Income			
Program	Number Assisted (Millions)	Elderly[a]	Disabled[b]	Able-Bodied, Nonelderly	With Children	Without Children	Pension, Social Security, SSI[c]	Work	TANF and State-Funded Cash Assistance[d]	Other[e]
					Percentage of Households					
HCV	2.2	21	28	51	48	52	50	28	12	11
PBRA	1.5	50	18	32	26	74	67	16	4	13
Public Housing	1.1	31	21	48	40	60	50	28	12	10
All Three										
Programs	4.8	32	23	44	39	61	55	24	9	11
					Millions of People					
HCV	5.2	0.6	1.1	3.4	3.7	1.5	1.9	1.9	0.8	0.6
PBRA	2.3	0.8	0.3	1.2	1.1	1.2	1.2	0.6	0.1	0.4
Public Housing	2.3	0.4	0.4	1.5	1.5	0.8	0.8	0.9	0.4	0.3
Total	9.8	1.9	1.8	6.1	6.3	3.5	3.8	3.3	1.4	1.4

Source: Congressional Budget Office based on data from the Department of Housing and Urban Development, Inventory Management System/PIH Information Center (IMS/PIC) and Tenant Rental Assistance Certification System (TRACS) (August 2014), and Department of Housing and Urban Development, FY 2013 Annual Performance Report and FY 2015 Annual Performance Plan (July 2014), p. 37, http://go.usa.gov/3F5uw.

Note: HCV = Housing Choice Voucher; PBRA = project-based rental assistance; SSI = Supplemental Security Income; TANF = Temporary Assistance for Needy Families.

[a] The head of the household, or his or her spouse, is age 62 or older.

[b] The nonelderly head of the household, or his or her spouse, is disabled.

[c] SSI guarantees a minimum amount of income for people who are elderly, blind, or disabled.

[d] State-funded cash assistance programs generally serve people without minor children who are not elderly and do not qualify for SSI.

[e] The category "Other" includes child support, medical reimbursement, Indian trust benefits, other nonwage sources, and unemployment benefits.

The household characteristics of people receiving indirect assistance through the LIHTC are not well documented. Currently, over 2 million LIHTC units exist for low-income households, but tenants may also receive other forms of federal low-income housing assistance. Studies examining a sample of households benefiting from that tax credit in the late 1990s indicated that tenants in those households had higher average income and were more likely to be working than people in households receiving direct assistance.[19]

Households That Do Not Receive Federal Assistance

About three-quarters of the roughly 20 million renter households that are eligible for direct housing assistance from the federal government do not receive it.[20] (The number of eligible households reflects those with income of no more than 50 percent of AMI—the limit primarily used to determine initial program eligibility for most of the direct assistance. It does not, however, include homeless people because it is difficult to obtain an accurate count of that population.) States also fund housing assistance programs but, compared with the federal government, direct a much smaller amount of spending to them—state programs tend to provide temporary help for people with mental illness or other disabilities, people who are homeless, or people at risk of becoming homeless.[21]

Most of the eligible but unassisted households (14 million in 2013) had rent expenditures that exceeded those of federally assisted households. That was the case for more than 80 percent of eligible but unassisted households with income equal to 50 percent or less of AMI. In contrast, the country's higher-income households spend a smaller share of their income on rent: Nearly half of households with income between 50 percent and 80 percent of AMI and about four-fifths of households with income exceeding 80 percent of AMI spend no more than 30 percent of their income on rent (see Figure 4).

Moreover, in 2013, 7.7 million households had what HUD describes as "worst-case housing needs," meaning that they had income of no more than 50 percent of AMI, were eligible for but did not receive federal housing assistance, and were paying more than half of their income in rent (or living in severely substandard conditions). That number was nearly 50 percent higher than a decade earlier but lower than the number in 2011 (see Figure 5). The trend in recent years reflects the influence of the recession and the ongoing recovery. About 35 percent of the households with worst-case housing needs in 2013 included children and nearly 20 percent included a head of household or spouse who was age 62 or older. The remaining 45 percent consisted mostly of nonelderly people living alone.[22]

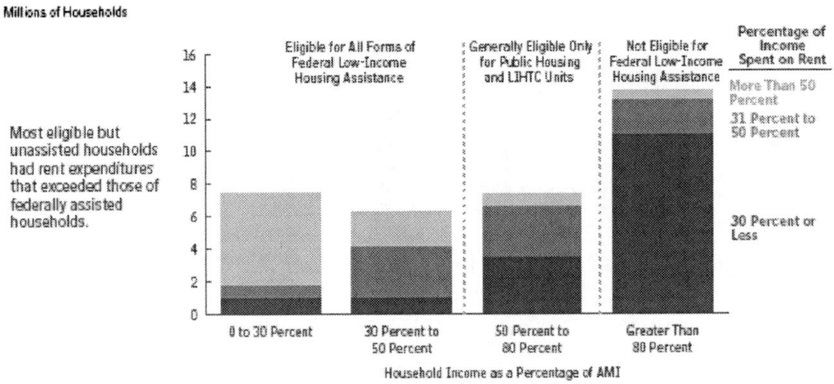

Source: Congressional Budget Office based on data from Department of Housing and Urban Development, Worst Case Housing Needs: 2015 Report to Congress (April 2015), Table A-1A, p. 30, www.huduser.org/portal/publications/affhsg/ wc_ HsgNeeds15.html.

Note: AMI = area median income; LIHTC = Low-Income Housing Tax Credit.

Figure 4. Households That Rent but Do Not Receive Federal Low-Income Housing Assistance, by Income and Rent Expenditure, 2013.

Households spending more of their income on housing have less to devote to other goods and services than people who spend less of their income for that purpose. Among households ranking in the lowest quarter of income in 2013, those spending more than 50 percent of their income on housing spent about three-fifths as much on food, about one-third as much on health care, and about one-third as much on transportation compared with those who spent 30 percent or less of their income on housing.[23] A 2014 survey of parents who spent more than 30 percent of household income on shelter found that, of the 75 percent making sacrifices to cover housing costs, about one-sixth had cut back on healthy food, about one-sixth had cut back on health care, about one-tenth had moved to a neighborhood that was less secure, and about one-tenth had moved to a neighborhood that had worse schools.[24]

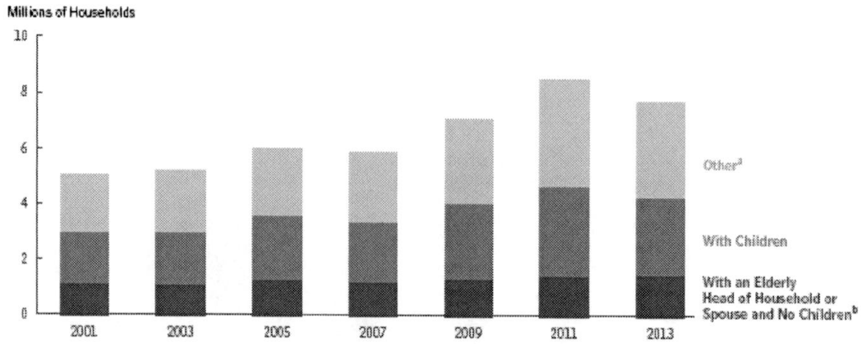

Source: Congressional Budget Office based on data from the Department of Housing and Urban Development, Worst Case Housing Needs: Reports to Congress (various years), www.huduser.org/portal/taxonomy/term/43.

Note: The Department of Housing and Urban Development (HUD) defines households with worst-case housing needs as those that have income of no more than 50 percent of area median income, are eligible for but do not receive federal housing assistance, and are paying more than half of their income in rent (or live in severely substandard conditions). Only about 3 percent of households characterized as having worst-case needs are identified as such solely because of substandard conditions; in all, about 6 percent of households with worst-case needs live in substandard conditions. In contrast to the data reflected in Table, data describing households with worst-case needs are collected in the Census Bureau's American Housing Survey, which does not offer consistent information over time about households with one or more disabled members.

[a]The category "Other" consists mostly of nonelderly people living alone.

[b] The head of the household, or his or her spouse, is age 62 or older.

Figure 5. Eligible Households That Did Not Receive Federal Low-Income Housing Assistance and Met HUD's Definition of "Worst-Case Housing Needs," 2001 to 2013.

Federal Housing Assistance and Employment

Federal housing programs, with limited exceptions, do not require that recipients engage in work-related activity. Like many programs that provide cash and in-kind benefits to low-income populations, federal housing assistance introduces incentives that tend to discourage employment. However, such assistance might also facilitate employment by providing housing stability and more opportunities. Ultimately, empirical studies find some reduction in work in response to federal housing assistance.

Work Requirements and Support for Work

For the most part, no work requirements or time limits are associated with receiving housing benefits.[25] In the public housing program, however, able-bodied tenants of working age, who are not working or are otherwise exempt, must participate in community service or self-sufficiency activities for eight hours per month. Residents who have not satisfied that requirement have an opportunity to do so; failure to comply can result in termination of assistance and eviction.

The voluntary Family Self-Sufficiency (FSS) program, established in 1990, provides federal support for participants who agree to work toward leaving the HCV program or public housing by increasing their earned income over a period of five years. Generally, subsidized tenants face a disincentive to increase their earnings because they pay a fixed percentage of their income toward rent. However, in the FSS program, any changes in household rent that are the result of a participant's growing income are credited to an escrow account that the tenant can use for any purpose when he or she successfully completes the program. Federally paid program coordinators work with private and public providers who help households plan for self-sufficiency by offering continuing education, job training, counseling, and other assistance, such as child care and transportation.

A 2009 study of the FSS program found that participants' average annual income increased by about 20 percent within four years compared with their income before participation. However, compared with others in the FSS program, participants in the study had higher income, employment rates, and educational attainment to begin with, and the study did not assess how their income would have changed if they had not participated in the program.[26] In March 2012, HUD commissioned an evaluation of the effectiveness of a variety of FSS programs in a diverse set of cities and local contexts; the results of that assessment are not yet available.[27]

Effects on Work. Housing assistance provides recipients with incentives that influence their willingness to work, in terms of both employment and the number of hours worked. Some incentives may discourage work and others may facilitate it.

One set of incentives tends to reduce the amount of time that people work. Housing assistance allows recipients of such benefits to maintain their standard of living while working less, an incentive known as the income effect. Because an increase in a household's income from working is partially offset by a reduction in the value of their housing benefits, housing assistance may also make spending time on activities other than work more desirable, which is termed the substitution effect. For example, if the monthly labor income of a household increased by $100, its housing benefits would be reduced by $30— the equivalent of a 30 percent marginal tax on earnings from work (but other policies might also affect people's effective marginal tax rate).[28] Because, on net, additional work provides less income than it would have otherwise, households have less incentive to work than they would have if they were not receiving assistance.

But in other ways, housing assistance may facilitate work. Housing assistance might encourage employment by providing a more stable housing arrangement for people with low income. If assistance reduces a household's spending on rent, that may facilitate work by freeing household resources for child care and transportation expenses. Housing assistance can also help people in low-income households move to areas closer to potential employers or to areas where neighbors can provide more contacts to potential employers.

Recent studies of housing assistance indicate that beneficiaries of housing assistance tend to work less. One study estimated that among able-bodied adults of working age, a housing choice voucher reduces employment, as measured by quarterly employment, by 6 percent and earnings, which are influenced by the number of hours worked, by 10 percent over a period of eight years; the size of the effects grew over time.[29] That study found no evidence that receiving a housing voucher increased residential stability or the proximity to employed neighbors.

Another study found that housing vouchers reduce recipients' employment by 5 percent to 8 percent and earnings by about 12 percent in the first year, but that the effects dissipated over time.[30] The authors attribute the first-year effects to the disruption of moving. The study used a comparatively small sample of households, all of which included people who were eligible for, were receiving, or had recently received TANF benefits. People who participate in both TANF and housing assistance programs may experience less of a disincentive to work than people who receive only housing assistance. That effect may arise because TANF provides families with cash assistance and other forms of support, such as child care, while encouraging states to have recipients engage in work-related activities.

A third study, which also included some households that had applied for or received TANF benefits, found no statistically significant change in employment over a five-year period; however, in the first year after receiving a voucher, household earnings declined by 12 percent. That reduction in earnings dissipated over time and was not statistically significant after five years.[31] Earlier studies examining the effect of housing assistance on work activity yielded mixed results, but many used methods of analysis that appear to result in statistical bias.

POLICY OPTIONS

Lawmakers could alter a number of features of federal housing assistance for low-income households in ways that would either expand such support, which in some cases would increase spending, or reduce such support, which in some cases would achieve budgetary savings. Aspects of low-income housing assistance that might be changed include:

- The size or composition of the assisted population,
- Tenants' contributions to rent,
- The resources available to PHAs, or
- The ways in which low-income housing assistance is provided.

CBO has estimated the budgetary effects of a number of such options over the 2016–2025 period (see Table 3).[32] Those effects, expressed in nominal dollars, range from 10-year savings of over $100 billion to 10-year costs of more than $400 billion.

Some options could be combined so as not to significantly alter budgetary expenditures. Policymakers could, for example, consider offsetting the cost of one policy (such as increasing the share of the low-income population that receives direct housing assistance) with another that generates savings (such as requiring assisted tenants to make a greater contribution toward rent or repealing the LIHTC). In structuring policies, lawmakers might also wish to consider other objectives, such as providing assistance to certain populations (for example, housing arrangements that might reduce homelessness), or designing policies that provide assistance without introducing incentives for low-income households to favor renting over homeownership.

Table 3. Policy Options for Federal Low-Income Housing Assistance and Estimated Budgetary Effects, 2016 to 2025

Policy Option	10-Year Budgetary Effects (Billions of dollars)
Change the Size or Composition of the Assisted Population	
Reduce the number of housing choice vouchers (HCVs)	
Reduce the number of HCVs by 10 percent	-18
Gradually eliminate HCVs for households with income over 30 percent of area median income (AMI)	-20
Gradually eliminate all HCVs	-118
Increase the number of HCVs	
Increase the number of HCVs by 10 percent	18
Gradually provide HCVs for all households with income of no more than 30 percent of AMI	290
Gradually provide HCVs for all eligible households	410
Require participation in a work support program and give priority to applicants who worka	10
Change Tenants' Contributions to Rent	
Increase the share of income that tenants pay in renta	-22
Reduce the share of income that tenants pay in renta	22
Change the Resources Available to Public Housing Agencies (PHAs)	
Increase PHAs' access to private fundsb	0
Require consolidation of PHAs and decrease funds for their administrative costs	No Estimate
Increase funds for the administration of housing assistance	4
Change the Ways in Which Assistance Is Provided	
Replace project-based rental assistance contracts with HCVs	No Estimate
Provide more money for the Housing Trust Fund to expand low-income housing	No Estimate
Repeal the Low-Income Housing Tax Credit	-42
Introduce a renter's tax credit	42

Sources: Congressional Budget Office and the staff of the Joint Committee on Taxation. Note: Estimates of the budgetary effects are expressed in nominal dollars.

[a] The option holds constant the number of households served.

[b] Because this option is designed to avoid creating obligation in advance of appropriations, it would be budget neutral.

Options That Would Change the Size or Composition of the Assisted Population

The resources currently provided to federal housing assistance programs for low-income households are not sufficient to serve all eligible households, and little distinction exists between the circumstances of the low-income households that are offered housing assistance and those that are not. Lawmakers could change the number of low-income households that receive housing assistance by reducing or increasing the number of vouchers provided in the HCV program, for example, or lawmakers could alter the composition of the population receiving aid by giving waiting-list priority to households with a working adult.

Reduce the Number of Housing Choice Vouchers

To illustrate ways to decrease costs associated with the HCV program, which accounted for $18 billion in federal spending in 2014, CBO analyzed the budgetary effects of reducing appropriations for the program by:

- Retiring 10 percent of all outstanding HCVs, by not reissuing them to new participants when households leave the program;
- Gradually restricting assistance to households with income of no more than 30 percent of AMI; or
- Eliminating all outstanding vouchers over a period of 10 years.

Retiring 10 percent of HCVs in 2016 would reduce federal spending by $18 billion from 2016 through 2025. A onetime reduction of that magnitude in the number of vouchers—about 190,000—could most likely be achieved without affecting households now served by the program. Tenants leave the HCV program each year, in some cases because of the dissolution of their family or because of a violation of program rules; in other cases, tenants leave because changing circumstances make them better off without a voucher. In 2013, roughly 300,000 voucher-subsidized households left the program. To the extent that sufficient funds are available, all of the vouchers that were used by households leaving the program are reissued to eligible households on waiting lists for federal housing subsidies. Hence, retiring HCVs would increase the amount of time that eligible but unassisted households would have to wait for a voucher. PHAs report that households newly assisted by the HCV program in 2013 had been waiting for assistance for an average of 23 months.[33] That figure probably understates the amount of time that households have to wait for assistance because many PHAs limit the size of their waiting lists by periodically closing them to new applicants.

Alternatively, lawmakers could gradually reduce the number of vouchers over a period of 10 years by retiring the vouchers of households with income of more than 30 percent of AMI as the tenants leave the program or have their vouchers canceled. Newly assisted households would be eligible for HCVs only if their income was no more than 30 percent of AMI. CBO estimates that such a policy change would reduce federal spending by $20 billion from 2016 through 2025. Such an approach would achieve budgetary savings without affecting the lowest-income households, but ultimately it would remove about half a million vouchers and an important source of support for tenants who, because of their higher income, might have been more likely to achieve self-sufficiency in the future had they received assistance.

Another option would be for lawmakers to end the program by eliminating all outstanding vouchers over a period of 10 years. Federal spending would be reduced by $118 billion from 2016 through 2025. Along with much larger budgetary savings than the options just discussed, this option would result in a much greater reduction in the resources available for the support of low-income households and, correspondingly, a greater increase in the possibility of overcrowding and homelessness: By 2025, about 2 million vouchers would be eliminated if the HCV program was terminated. An unresolved question is whether the substantial decrease in spending on housing assistance would lower unsubsidized rents, including those paid by low-income households, by reducing demand for housing. Very few empirical studies are available that examine the effect of vouchers on rents. This report summarizes the existing research—most of which suggests that the number of vouchers does not affect overall rents—in the following discussion about increasing the number of vouchers.

Increase the Number of Housing Choice Vouchers

Lawmakers could also choose to spend more money and assist more people, for example, by:

- Increasing the number of available vouchers by 10 percent,
- Offering assistance to all households with income of no more than 30 percent of AMI, or
- Offering assistance to all households with income of no more than 50 percent of AMI.

Regardless of the size of the increase in the number of available vouchers, more households that would not receive assistance under the current program, even though they are eligible for it, would be served—but at an added cost. CBO estimates that a onetime 10 percent increase in the number of vouchers would assist roughly 200,000 additional households and cause federal spending to increase by a total of $18 billion from 2016 through 2025. Offering vouchers gradually over a period of 10 years to all households with income of no more than 30 percent of AMI would ultimately assist roughly 4.5 million additional households at a cost of $290 billion from 2016 through 2025. Offering vouchers to all households with income of no more than 50 percent of AMI would ultimately assist about 8 million additional households and would cause federal spending to increase by $410 billion from 2016 through 2025.[34]

In addition to the cost, another drawback is that providing more vouchers might lead to higher rents by increasing demand for housing. Rent increases would mean that subsidies from the voucher program were to some extent accruing to property owners instead of assisted households, and those increases could also affect rents paid by low-income households that do not receive assistance. The limited research on this question, including some of the most recent work, suggests that an increase in the number of vouchers might not affect the overall rents for dwellings comparable to the subsidized units.[35] However, one study found that additional vouchers could affect rents for some units in the near term, depending on the rent charged for a unit before the voucher expansion.[36] According to that analysis, when additional vouchers were provided in areas where the housing supply was relatively inflexible, units for which the rent had been near the maximum allowed by HUD had rents that moved closer to that maximum. That study suggested that newly assisted households increase their demand for higher-quality units (those with rents near the maximum allowable amount for the HCV program) and decrease their demand for lower-quality units. An earlier analysis also found that increases in the number of vouchers in the mid-1970s through the mid-1990s were associated with rent increases for unsubsidized households in the lowest-income neighborhoods, but that analysis did not account for other factors that may have explained the rent increases—such as changes in the quality of rental units over that period.[37]

Require Participation in a Work Support Program and Give Waiting-List Priority to Applicants Who Work

For the most part, no work requirements are associated with the federal government's low-income housing assistance and that assistance is not targeted specifically to the working poor. Lawmakers could make participation in the Family Self-Sufficiency program mandatory for able-bodied heads of households of working age who receive direct housing assistance—of whom there are approximately 2.1 million. If successful completion of that program led to their departure from assisted housing, lawmakers could require PHAs to offer that assistance to people on the waiting list who are already working and thus might be more likely to achieve self-sufficiency.

If the federal government expanded the FSS program and changed the waiting-list policy for PHAs, while holding constant the overall number of assisted households, net federal spending would increase by about $10 billion from 2016 through 2025, CBO estimates. The estimated cost includes $12 billion in greater federal spending to compensate staff who develop FSS contracts, help participants obtain jobs and services, provide ongoing case management, and maintain escrow accounts. The estimated budgetary effect also reflects $2 billion in federal costs associated with the rent payments that PHAs would usually retain but instead would put in escrow accounts held for the tenants when tenants' incomes increased. (CBO is unaware of research that demonstrates that participating in the program affects participants' income; therefore, the estimate does not include such an effect.) Finally, the estimated budgetary effect reflects $4 billion in federal savings associated with replacing FSS participants who leave the housing assistance programs with households that include working adults. Such households have higher income and therefore make larger rent payments than the average household receiving assistance under current law.

An advantage of giving waiting-list preference to households with employed adults is that the assistance might enable those households to ultimately become self-sufficient. In addition, such an approach would free up resources to serve more of the eligible population. It would also introduce an incentive for members of households not receiving assistance to seek employment and thereby move up on the PHA's waiting list for housing assistance. But a disadvantage of awarding more housing assistance to tenants who work is that it would divert support from lower-income households that are also eligible for such assistance, households whose other housing options might be worse than those of the higher-income households. Moreover, a key difficulty with expanding FSS is placing participants in jobs that pay enough to allow them to become more self-sufficient. Another challenge is that the FSS program relies on organizations that provide services—such as child care, transportation, and adult education—to help participants increase their income, but support for these organizations is sometimes unstable, which might limit the services that the FSS program can access. If access to those services was reduced, FSS participants could find it more difficult to acquire the skills and support that would help them become self-sufficient.

Options That Would Change Tenants' Contributions to Rent

To save money, lawmakers could require that tenants who receive housing assistance pay a larger share of their income toward rent. Alternatively, to provide greater support to assisted households, lawmakers could allow tenants who receive housing assistance to pay a smaller share of their income toward rent. In 1968, lawmakers stipulated that households would pay no more than 25 percent of income toward rent in federally assisted housing; in 1981, that payment amount was increased to 30 percent of household income. CBO has estimated the budgetary effects of changing that percentage to 35 percent or 25 percent. Other options that could be designed to increase or decrease tenants' total contributions toward rent include establishing tiered rents that are based on income or household status—specifically, whether the household is headed by an elderly, disabled, or nonelderly and nondisabled person—or establishing flat rents that are unrelated to income. CBO did not estimate the budgetary effects of such alternatives.

Increase the Share of Income That Tenants Pay in Rent

Together, the three direct assistance programs—HCV, PBRA, and public housing—accounted for $36 billion in federal spending in 2014. To reduce such spending, lawmakers could gradually increase payments made by tenants who participate in those programs from 30 percent to 35 percent of adjusted household income over a period of five years. Doing so, while holding constant the number of participants, would reduce spending by $22 billion from 2016 through 2025. This option would reduce the preferential treatment accorded to low-income households that receive federal rental assistance. Most renters who are eligible for, but do not receive, federal low-income housing assistance pay more than 30 percent of their income in rent. Only about one in seven unassisted renters with the lowest income (30 percent or less of AMI) and one in six of those with somewhat higher income (between 30 percent and 50 percent of AMI) paid 30 percent or less of their income in rent in 2013.

One disadvantage of this option is that assisted households would have fewer resources to support other purchases, such as those associated with food, health care, and transportation. Another disadvantage is that the increase in the effective marginal tax on tenants' earnings would discourage work.

Reduce the Share of Income That Tenants Pay in Rent

To increase the support to households in the HCV, PBRA, and public housing programs, lawmakers could gradually decrease tenants' payments from 30 percent to 25 percent of adjusted household income over a period of five years. Doing so, while holding constant the number of participants, would increase spending by $22 billion from 2016 through 2025.

This option would benefit some low-income tenants who receive direct housing assistance—many of whom are in poverty—by reducing their expenditures on rent, giving them more resources to support other purchases. Also, the reduction in the effective marginal tax rate on tenants' earnings would encourage work. However, this option would increase the preferential treatment accorded to low-income households that receive federal rental assistance and would have no effect on the many households that are eligible for but do not receive assistance; about three-quarters of those households with income no higher than 30 percent of AMI devote more than half of their income toward rent.

Options That Would Change the Resources Available to PHAs

A number of housing assistance properties, both publicly and privately owned, could benefit from rehabilitation. According to HUD's estimates from

2010, potential capital expenditures to repair and replace items (such as windows, kitchens, bathrooms, and roofs) and to enhance energy and water efficiency at public housing properties were about $25 billion (in 2010 dollars) and projected to grow at a rate of $3 billion annually.[38] Lawmakers could increase PHAs' access to private funds for capital spending. Lawmakers could also consider whether consolidation of PHAs would yield desirable administrative efficiencies that could be combined with reduced appropriations. In addition, lawmakers could consider whether to appropriate amounts sufficient to fully provide for the formula-determined payments that support PHAs' administrative responsibilities.

Increase PHAs' Access to Private Funds

Lawmakers could, without affecting the federal budget, augment PHAs' ability to borrow money from private sources by allowing them to pledge a greater share of future appropriations to repaying loans. At present, with approval from HUD, a PHA can borrow private capital to develop or modernize public housing by pledging no more than one-third of its expected future capital fund appropriations to debt-service payments.[39] From fiscal year 2000 through the end of fiscal year 2015, HUD had approved the allocation of $4.5 billion (in nominal dollars) to debt-service payments through the Capital Fund Financing Program.[40]

The advantage of borrowing from the private sector in this way is that it enables PHAs to obtain capital for public housing improvements sooner. Enabling them to do more such borrowing could increase the long-term efficiency of capital spending by preventing significant physical deterioration that would ultimately be more costly to repair. Such borrowing has trade-offs, however: More of the funds appropriated in the future would be committed to the repayment of loans, and the pressure to maintain or increase such funding would be greater. Moreover, because the pledge of repayment is subject to the future appropriation of funds by the Congress (the federal government neither guarantees nor provides full faith and credit for these transactions), there is no assurance that funds sufficient to repay the loans would be appropriated in future years; HUD's approvals for borrowing and the costs of such borrowing would have to reflect that uncertainty.

Lawmakers could also increase access to private funds by authorizing an expansion of the Rental Assistance Demonstration Program. Under that program, PHAs convert public housing to project-based rental assistance or to project-based HCVs. The property owners can then renovate or redevelop the units using private sources of financing—such as conventional mortgages—and the LIHTC. By the end of 2014, HUD had received applications for the conversion of more than 176,000 units but had authority to approve the conversion of only 60,000 units.[41]

An advantage of this option is its potential for improving the condition of properties used to provide housing assistance. One drawback of the option is that the potential for expanding the program might be limited by the number of public housing properties that were capable of attracting private investment.

Require Consolidation of PHAs and Decrease Funds for Their Administrative Costs

Lawmakers could require PHAs—particularly smaller ones—that serve related or adjacent rental markets to consolidate their operations. Consolidation could generate budgetary savings because lawmakers appropriate funds for PHAs, in part, on the basis of the costs associated with administering housing units. The administrative duties of PHAs, such as those associated with managing waiting lists, hiring inspectors, and preparing and submitting financial reports to the federal government, might be executed at lower cost if PHAs benefited from economies of scale by joining together.

The data suggest that potential candidates for consolidation exist. More than 800 PHAs in metropolitan areas each administer fewer than 250 low-income housing units, as do almost 1,500 PHAs in nonmetropolitan areas. In both cases, at least 20 percent of those small PHAs are not the only ones in their area.

The Congress has recently taken steps to encourage the consolidation of some PHA operations.[42] However, CBO has not estimated the associated reductions in federal spending because of a lack of sufficient information. One potential disadvantage of consolidation is that PHAs risk losing local control and discretion over housing programs.

Increase Funding for PHAs' Administration of Housing Assistance

Over the past decade, appropriations for the administration of housing assistance have been less than the amounts indicated by the funding formula—

averaging about 80 percent of those amounts.[43] If lawmakers were to appropriate amounts sufficient to fully provide the formula-determined payments that support PHAs' administrative responsibilities (see Box 1), doing so—while holding constant the number of households served—would increase federal spending by $4 billion from 2016 to 2025 compared with maintaining funding, in real terms, at its 2014 level.

One potential advantage of such a policy change is that adequate funding for PHAs' administrative tasks would help housing support programs run more smoothly—by minimizing delays in the processing of new participants or in the inspections required before a unit is occupied, for example. The formula amounts outlined in appropriation acts aim to take into account changes in administrative costs over time. In recent years, as administrative funding has fallen below formula amounts, PHAs have pointed to rising costs (associated with increased voucher portability, additional reporting and other requirements, and employees' health care) as evidence of the need for increased funding.[44] A potential disadvantage of implementing such a policy, however, is that the formula amount for administrative payments might not accurately reflect the costs to PHAs of efficiently performing their required tasks.[45]

Options That Would Change the Ways in Which Assistance Is Provided

Lawmakers could also explore whether housing assistance would be delivered more effectively by shifting support toward certain programs, eliminating programs, or introducing new programs. For instance, policymakers could replace PBRA contracts with HCVs, provide more money to the states through the Housing Trust Fund, repeal the LIHTC, or introduce a renter's tax credit.

Replace PBRA Contracts with HCVs

Lawmakers could stop appropriating funds for the renewal of contracts for project-based rental assistance and provide tenants with vouchers instead. On the basis of the limited available evidence about the extent to which PBRA rents or HCV rents are above market rates, it is unclear whether replacing PBRA contracts with HCVs would generate significant savings.[46] It is generally acknowledged that some of the original long-term PBRA contracts involved rents that exceeded market levels. By one estimate, about 4,500 of the original PBRA contracts involved above-market rents.[47] However, most of the original long-term contracts have expired. Currently, only about 1,200 of the approximately 17,000 existing PBRA contracts are funded from long-term appropriations, and almost all of those long-term contracts (some of which may involve above-market rents) will expire by the end of 2021.[48]

Further, evidence of above-market rents among longterm contracts that have not yet expired is limited. The federal Mark-to-Market program was enacted to reduce the subsidy costs for most PBRA properties as the original contracts came up for renewal. As of the summer of 2003, owners of nearly 1,200 properties had successfully completed the process for the Mark-to-Market program; of those, less than 20 percent (representing no more than 5 percent of the total units in the Mark-to-Market program) received authorization to charge above-market rents (to maintain operations in areas with shortages of low-income housing). On average, those "exception rents" were about 20 percent above market rents.[49]

A potential advantage of using HCVs to replace PBRA contracts is that annual rent increases might be subject to greater market discipline. In the HCV program, a rent increase requested by a property owner goes into effect only if the PHA approves it as reasonable on the basis of rents for comparable private market units in the area. Rent increases in the PBRA program are generally based on an operating cost adjustment factor, which is currently calculated for each state by HUD, using publicly available indexes, as the sum of weighted average changes in costs for wages, employees' benefits, property taxes, insurance, supplies and equipment, fuel oil, electricity, natural gas, and water, sewer, and trash services.[50] In some years, however, rent increases for some PBRA properties may reflect market rates as determined by a rent comparability study conducted every five years.[51]

A potential disadvantage of ending project-based rental assistance in favor of housing choice vouchers is that it could reduce the supply of low-income housing. The existence of PBRA units for low-income households is guaranteed for the term of the contract, regardless of changes in the area's housing costs. In contrast, landlords in strong housing markets might not have sufficient incentives to accept vouchers. Project-based rental assistance might also better facilitate the production of low-income housing for people who could benefit from concentrated services, such as the elderly or people with disabilities. Another possible disadvantage of not renewing PBRA contracts—and providing tenants with vouchers instead—is the risk that such a policy could impose additional costs on the federal government. Specifically, making such a change could reduce the number of assisted tenants in project-based properties, and those that could not attract enough unassisted tenants could default on federally insured loans (such as those held by most of the roughly 2,500 properties that, to date, have undergone rent reductions and mortgage restructurings in the Mark-to-Market program).[52]

Provide More Money for the Housing Trust Fund to Expand Low-Income Housing

Providing a fixed amount of mandatory funding for the Housing Trust Fund (HTF) would result in a commensurate increase in federal spending beyond the roughly $3 billion that CBO estimates will result from contributions made by Fannie Mae and Freddie Mac over the 2016–2025 period. (Expressed in 2014 dollars, the average subsidy for households receiving assistance through the HCV program, PBRA, or public housing in 2013 was $7,700.) The HTF is for use by state-designated grant recipients to preserve or produce low-income housing. Under current law, 80 percent of such a grant must be used for rental housing. (Up to 10 percent can be used to support homeownership and up to 10 percent can be used for administrative and planning costs.) At least 75 percent of the funds for rental housing must benefit households with income at or below 30 percent of AMI (a condition that applies in other low-income housing assistance programs) or income at or below the federal poverty level. Regulations set the maximum rent for the subsidized units differently depending on a household's income. If a household's income is no greater than 30 percent of AMI, maximum rent is the greater of 30 percent of the FPL or 9 percent of AMI. If a household's income exceeds 30 percent of AMI but not 50 percent of AMI, maximum rent is 15 percent of AMI. Such rent restrictions have to remain in place for at least 30 years.[53]

An advantage of providing additional money for the HTF is that it would allow the federal government to assist more of the eligible low-income population. In addition, the HTF is the only active federal spending program that supports creating new units for low-income households, given that lawmakers repealed the authority to use PBRA funds for new construction or the substantial rehabilitation of housing units over 30 years ago. Project-based subsidies might help preserve low-income units in areas where landlords are less willing to accept HCVs because of growing strength in the housing market.

A potential disadvantage of providing assistance through the HTF is that the housing it would support could be difficult to afford for those earning substantially less than 30 percent of AMI, in contrast with direct assistance programs (such as the voucher program) in which tenants' rent contributions are determined on the basis of an individual household's income. Thus, certain low-income households might require additional forms of assistance to be able to benefit from assistance provided through the HTF.

Repeal the LIHTC

According to an estimate by JCT, repealing the Low-Income Housing Tax Credit would increase revenues by $42 billion from 2016 through 2025.[54]

One advantage of relying less on the LIHTC would be that other methods of supporting the provision of low-income housing are more effective in economic downturns and thus less susceptible to fluctuations in macroeconomic conditions. For example, with the collapse of the housing market during the recent economic downturn, the investors that bought the most tax credits—large banks, Fannie Mae, and Freddie Mac— incurred substantial losses that reduced their taxable income and limited their ability to take tax credits. The decline in the market value of the credits made it harder for developers to obtain project financing at a time when several factors, such as increased unemployment and home foreclosures, heightened the demand for low-income housing.

A disadvantage of repealing the LIHTC is that those credits could offer advantages over vouchers in helping to preserve low-income units for the term of the contract even in areas that experience growing strength in their housing markets. As areas become more desirable, landlords might be less willing to accept vouchers. In addition, by helping to produce and preserve low-income rental housing, the LIHTC can help improve neighborhoods.[55] For example, one study of LIHTC developments completed between 1991 and 2000 in New York City found that the use of LIHTCs to replace abandoned buildings and construct buildings on empty lots in blighted neighborhoods led to increased property values within a few blocks of the newly constructed buildings' location. Although the positive effects diminished somewhat over time, they remained significant five years after completion of the projects.[56]

An unresolved question in evaluating the effects of the LIHTC is whether, by subsidizing providers of housing instead of households, it represents a relatively costly way to provide for low-income housing. Although the evidence is limited, one study of the LIHTC in one medium-sized metropolitan area estimated that about one-third of the subsidy provided through the credit translated into savings on rent for low-income households, and two-thirds of the subsidy was kept by housing providers.[57]

Introduce a Renter's Tax Credit

If lawmakers wished to expand support for low-income housing, they could establish federal tax credits for renters with low income. For example, introducing a renter's tax credit that was designed to cost the same as the LIHTC would reduce tax receipts by $42 billion from 2016 through 2025.

The advantage of a renter's tax credit, which would provide assistance similar to that offered through the HCV program, is that it could allow tenants to rent a unit of their choice in the private market. As with a voucher, the nonrefundable credit could be transferred to property owners—many of whom would have sufficient tax liability to claim the credits. A property owner could also pass the credit through to a mortgage lender in exchange for reduced mortgage payments. That would allow entities that do not pay taxes—such as nonprofits, real estate investment trusts, and pension funds—to participate.

A potential disadvantage of this option is that the administrative costs would be greater than those of providing housing assistance through vouchers. Eligibility determinations could be handled by public housing agencies in the same way under both approaches, but claimants would have more complicated tax filings and the government's administration of the tax code would be more complicated, especially if the tax credits were transferred to third parties. In addition, the budgetary costs of providing assistance through a renter's tax credit would be less transparent than the costs of providing housing assistance through appropriations for the HCV program. Because tax expenditures appear in the federal budget in the form of reduced revenues rather than increased spending, they make the budget and scope of the government's activities appear smaller.

Appendix: Federal Support for Housing That Is Not Focused on Low-Income Households

In addition to providing support for low-income housing, the federal government also provides support for housing in general. Most of that assistance is made available through provisions in the tax code—deductions, exclusions, and excess depreciation—that primarily benefit households with higher income. Moreover, the federal government provides mortgage assistance through loan guarantees and insurance.[1]

Tax Expenditures

Together, tax-code provisions that support housing resulted in estimated tax expenditures of $130 billion in 2014 (see Table A-1).[2] Tax expenditures resemble government spending programs by providing financial assistance to specific activities, entities, or groups of people.

Tax Deduction for Mortgage Interest

The federal tax deduction for mortgage interest payments accounted for about $68 billion in tax expenditures in 2014, according to an estimate by the staff of the Joint Committee on Taxation (JCT).[3] The deduction is limited to payments on the first $1 million of a household's mortgage debt and $100,000 for other debt (such as a home-equity loan).

Relative to other taxpayers, lower-income households receive the least benefit from the current itemized deduction, for several reasons. First, taxpayers with lower income are more likely to be renters than are taxpayers with higher income, who are more likely to be homeowners. Second, lower-income households are less likely than higher-income households to have sufficient deductions to make itemizing worthwhile; for taxpayers with only small amounts of deductions that can be itemized, the standard deduction—which is a flat dollar amount—provides a larger tax benefit. Third, the value of itemized deductions is greater for people in the higher income tax brackets. And fourth, the value of the mortgage interest deduction is greater for people who have larger mortgages.

Dividing the nation's households into five groups of equal size, arrayed by before-tax income, the Congressional Budget Office estimates that households in the top quintile received about three-fourths of the benefit of the mortgage interest deduction in 2013. Those in the quintile just below received most of the rest of such benefits (see Table A-2). Only a small percentage of the benefit went to households in the middle quintile, and even those households had income that was about four times greater than the average income of households receiving means-tested federal housing assistance.

Table A-1. Tax Expenditures That Are Not Focused on Low-Income Housing, 2014

Federal Tax Provision	Estimated Tax Expenditure (Billions of dollars)
Deduction for Mortgage Interest	68
Deduction for Property Taxes	32
Exclusion From Taxable Income of Capital Gains on Sales of Principal Residences	24
Depreciation of Rental Housing in Excess of the Alternative Depreciation System[a]	5
Exclusion From Taxable Income of Interest on Qualified Private Activity Bonds for Owner-Occupied Housing	1
Deduction for Mortgage Insurance Premiums	1
Total[b]	130

Source: Congressional Budget Office based on data from the staff of the Joint Committee on Taxation, Estimates of Federal Tax Expenditures for Fiscal Years 2014–2018 (August 2014), www.jct.gov/publications.html?func=select&id=5.

[a] Under the alternative depreciation system, the income tax deduction—which acknowledges the deterioration of residential rental property—may be evenly distributed over a period of 40 years.

[b] The total tax expenditure estimate does not take into account interactions between individual provisions.

Tax Deduction for Property Taxes

The federal tax deduction for property taxes accounted for about $32 billion in tax expenditures in 2014, according to estimates by JCT.

Homeowners who itemize deductions can deduct from their federal taxes the local (or state) property taxes that they pay on their homes. As with the federal tax deduction for mortgage interest, lower-income households generally receive a smaller benefit from this deduction than those with higher income.

Exclusion of Capital Gains on Sales of Principal Residences

This exclusion accounted for about $24 billion in federal tax expenditures in 2014, according to estimates by JCT. Generally, when taxpayers sell assets they pay capital gains taxes on any profits they realize from the sale; but homeowners can exclude from their taxable income up to $250,000 ($500,000 if they file jointly) in capital gains on the sale of their house if it has been their principal residence for two of the preceding five years and if they have not claimed this exclusion for the sale of a different home during the preceding two years. As with the previous two types of federal support for homebuyers provided through the tax system, lower-income households generally receive a smaller benefit from this exclusion than taxpayers with higher income and more expensive homes.

Depreciation of Rental Housing in Excess of the Alternative Depreciation System

JCT estimates that excess depreciation for rental housing accounted for about $5 billion in tax expenditures in 2014.

Depreciation is an income tax deduction that acknowledges the deterioration of most types of tangible property used for business or investment by allowing a taxpayer to recover the cost (or other basis) of that property. Under the Alternative Depreciation System, residential rental property would be depreciated in equal amounts over a period of 40 years. However, residential rental property owners typically use the General Depreciation System, which provides for the depreciation to be evenly distributed over a shorter period of 27.5 years. CBO did not attempt to assess how this provision affects lower-income households.

Exclusion of Interest Earned on Qualified Private Activity Bonds for Owner-Occupied Housing

The exclusion from taxable income of interest on qualified private activity bonds for owner-occupied housing accounted for $1.2 billion in tax expenditures in 2014, according to estimates by JCT. Such bonds (known as single-family mortgage revenue bonds or qualified mortgage bonds) are issued by state and local governments to finance mortgage loans on single-family homes.

Tax Deduction for Mortgage Insurance Premiums

The federal tax deduction for mortgage insurance premiums accounted for $0.6 billion in tax expenditures in 2014, according to estimates by JCT. Premiums are fully deductible for taxpayers with adjusted gross income of no more than $100,000; however, the deduction phases out for taxpayers with income of more than $100,000, and those with income of more than $109,000 are not eligible for the deduction.[4] This provision expired at the end of 2014.

Table A-2. Mortgage Interest Deduction: Share of Tax Expenditures by Income Group, 2013

Quintile	Percent
Highest	73
Fourth	18
Middle	6
Second	2
Lowest	*

Source: Congressional Budget Office. For more information, see The Distribution of Major Tax Expenditures in the Individual Income Tax System (May 2013), Table 2, www.cbo.gov/publication/43768.

Note: * = between zero and 0.5 percent.

MORTGAGE LOAN GUARANTEES AND INSURANCE

In addition to the support provided through the tax code, the federal government provides mortgage assistance through loan guarantees (Fannie

Mae and Freddie Mac are the largest providers of those guarantees) and mortgage insurance.

Mortgage Loan Guarantees

Fannie Mae and Freddie Mac, originally chartered as government-sponsored enterprises, were established to ensure a stable supply of credit for residential mortgages nationwide. They buy mortgages from financial institutions that make such loans, thus ensuring that those institutions have funds to originate new mortgages. Fannie Mae and Freddie Mac pool the loans they purchase to create mortgage-backed securities to sell to investors and guarantee those securities against defaults on principal and interest payments by borrowers.

In 2013, CBO projected that Fannie Mae and Freddie Mac would issue about $1.2 trillion in loan guarantees in 2014, with a subsidy cost to the government of $6.7 billion over the lifetime of those loans.[5] CBO's estimates are measured on a fair-value basis—an accounting procedure that comprehensively reflects the cost to the government.[6]

Mortgage Insurance

The Federal Housing Administration (FHA) provides insurance for single-family and multifamily home mortgages issued by private lenders to borrowers who lack the savings, credit history, or income to qualify for conventional mortgages. According to the rules for budgetary accounting prescribed in the Federal Credit Reform Act of 1990, insurance on mortgages issued in 2014 and 2015 for single-family homes will produce estimated budgetary savings of about $16 billion. In contrast, on a fair-value basis, the insurance will cost the government an estimated $2 billion. The fair-value measure of the cost of that insurance more comprehensively accounts for the subsidy that is accruing to mortgage lenders and homeowners who have insured mortgages.[7] The Census Bureau reports that in 2013, only 6 percent of owner-occupied housing units with FHA mortgage insurance had income below federal poverty guidelines.[8]

NOTES

Numbers in the text and tables may not add up to totals because of rounding.

Unless otherwise indicated, all years referred to in the text, tables, and figures are federal fiscal years (which run from October 1 to September 30). Dollar values, with the exception of those describing 10-year budgetary effects, are expressed in 2014 dollars—unless otherwise specified—and have been adjusted to remove the effects of inflation using the gross domestic product price index. Ten-year budgetary effects are expressed in nominal dollars.

Unless otherwise noted, a low-income household is one with income that is no greater than 80 percent of the median income in a given area.\

End Notes

[1]. Information about the number of low-income households that receive, or do not receive, federal housing assistance and the characteristics of those households is based on data from 2013, the most recent year for which such data are available.

[2] See Joint Committee on Taxation, *Estimates of Federal Tax Expenditures for Fiscal Years 2014–2018*, JCX-97-14 (August 2014), www.jct.gov/ publications.html?func=select&id=5.

[3] Estimates of tax expenditures are based on people's behavior with the provisions in place and do not reflect how people would adjust their activities in response to changes in the tax code. Thus, the estimates do not reflect the amount of revenue that would be raised if those provisions were eliminated from the tax code. Also, the total amount of the tax expenditures does not take into account interactions between individual provisions of the tax code.

[4] The commonly used term "Section 8" housing refers to assistance programs authorized by section 8 of the Housing Act of 1937, which provide payments on behalf of assisted tenants to owners of private buildings. Accordingly, Section 8 assistance encompasses both the Housing Choice Voucher program and project-based rental assistance; nonetheless, some people use it to refer solely to the HCV program.

[5] For more information, see Department of Housing and Urban Development, *Housing Choice Voucher Program Guidebook* (April 2001), Chapters 6 and 7, http://go.usa.gov/3ZZr3.

[6] For further details, see Department of Housing and Urban Development, "Renewal of Section 8 Project-Based Rental Assistance" (accessed September 3, 2015), http://go.usa.gov/ 3ZZrT.

[7] 42 U.S.C. §1437f(c)(8)(A) (2012).

[8] For more information, see Department of Housing and Urban Development, *Public Housing Occupancy Guidebook* (June 2003), p. 130, http://go.usa.gov/3ZZNk.

[9] For more information, see Office of the Comptroller of the Currency, "Low-Income Housing Tax Credits: Affordable Housing Investment Opportunities for Banks" (March 2014), http://go.usa.gov/39VSd (PDF, 657 KB).

[10] See Department of Housing and Urban Development, "Low-Income Housing Tax Credits" (accessed September 3, 2015), www.huduser. org/portal/ datasets/lihtc.html.

[11] The payment calculation depends on whether the property owner, in qualifying for the credit, chooses to reserve at least 20 percent of the units for households with income at or below 50 percent of AMI or at least 40 percent of the units for households with income at or below 60 percent of AMI.

[12] For information about households receiving direct assistance, see Katherine M. O'Regan and Keren M. Horn, "What Can We Learn About the Low Income Housing Tax Credit Program by Looking at the Tenants?" *Housing Policy Debate*, vol. 23, no. 3 (May 2013), pp. 597–613, http://dx.doi.org/ 10.1080/10511482.2013.772909. For information about rent determination, see Project-Based Voucher Rents for Units Receiving Low-Income Housing Tax Credits, 72 Fed. Reg. 65206 (November 19, 2007), and Department of Housing and Urban Development, "Calculating Rent for Units with Low-Income Housing Tax Credit Allocations Combined With Housing Choice Voucher Assistance Under the Tenant-Based and Project-Based Programs" (November 1, 2002), www.novoco.com/ low_income_ housing/lihtc/other_guidance.php.

[13] A private activity bond is a tax-exempt bond that is issued by or on behalf of a local or state government to finance the project of a private business. Bondholders do not have to pay federal (and often state) income taxes on the interest associated with the bond.

[14] The allocation is 65 percent of an amount equal to 4.2 basis points for each dollar of the unpaid principal balance. See sec. 1337 and 1338 of the Housing and Economic Recovery Act of 2008, Public Law 110-289, 122 Stat. 2654, 2711.

[15]. See Housing Trust Fund Proposed Rule, 75 Fed. Reg. 209 (October 29, 2010) and Federal Housing Finance Agency, "FHFA Statement on the Housing Trust Fund and Capital Magnet Fund" (press release, December 11, 2014), http://go.usa.gov/3BUk5.

[16]. See Mihir Desai, Dhammika Dharmapala, and Monica Singhal, "Tax Incentives for Affordable Housing: The Low Income Housing Tax Credit," in Jeffrey R. Brown, ed., *Tax Policy and the Economy,* vol. 24 (University of Chicago Press, August 2010), pp. 181–205, www.nber.org/ chapters/c11971.pdf (452 KB); Steven Maguire, *Tax-Exempt Bonds: A Description of State and Local Government Debt,* Report for Congress RL30638 (Congressional Research Service, June 19, 2012), p. 14; and Government Accountability Office, *Low-Income Housing Tax Credits: Agencies Implemented Changes Enacted in 2008, but Project Data Collection Could Be Improved,* GAO-13-66 (December 6, 2012), www.gao.gov/products/GAO-13-66.

[17]. See Department of Housing and Urban Development, "FY 2013 Income Limits" (effective December 11, 2012), www.huduser.org/ portal/datasets/il/il13/index.html. HUD's income determination generally takes into account the income of all adult household members, including cash assistance provided through Temporary Assistance for Needy Families, and any unearned income attributable to a minor, such as child support and TANF payments. It does not include in-kind benefits, such as those provided through SNAP or Medicaid. The HUD income limits specified in this paper are for a four-person household; that information forms the basis for HUD's calculation of income limits for other household sizes. Amounts in this section are expressed in 2013 dollars to facilitate direct comparison with the published benchmarks and the most recently available demographic data for assisted households.

[18]. See Department of Health and Human Services, "Annual Update of the HHS Poverty Guidelines" (January 24, 2013), http://go.usa.gov/3BUuz. Alaska and Hawaii have separate guidelines.

[19]. See General Accounting Office (now the Government Accountability Office), *Tax Credits: Opportunities to Improve Oversight of the Low-Income Housing Program,* GAO/GGD/

RCED-97-55 (March 28, 1997), www.gao. gov/products/GGD/ RCED-97-55; and Department of Housing and Urban Development, *Assessment of the Economic and Social Characteristics of LIHTC Residents and Neighborhoods* (prepared by Abt Associates, February 2000), Exhibits 3-4 and 3-19, www.abtassociates.com/reports/ 20008744902172.pdf (458 KB).

[20] See Department of Housing and Urban Development, *Worst Case Housing Needs: 2015 Report to Congress* (May 1, 2015), Table A-1A, www.huduser. org/portal/ publications/affhsg/ wc_HsgNeeds15.html.

[21] See Rachel Bergquist and others, *State Funded Housing Assistance Programs* (Technical Assistance Collaborative, April 2014), http://tinyurl. com/neze642.

[22]. See Department of Housing and Urban Development, *Worst Case Housing Needs: 2015 Report to Congress* (May 1, 2015), Table A-1A, www.huduser. org/portal/ publications/affhsg/ wc_HsgNeeds15.html.

[23] See Joint Center for Housing Studies of Harvard University, *The State of the Nation's Housing 2015* (2015), Table A-3, www.jchs. harvard.edu/research/ state_nations_housing.

[24] See MacArthur Foundation, "How Housing Matters: The Housing Crisis Continues to Loom Large in the Experiences and Attitudes of the American Public" (prepared by Hart Research Associates, April 2014), p. 21, http://tinyurl.com/pbbs3bo (PDF, 1.15 MB).

[25]. A few PHAs do, however, have the authority to impose such requirements. The Moving to Work program allows for exemptions from most federal housing rules to help achieve the program's goals, and some of the roughly 40 participating PHAs are experimenting with rent and eligibility rules to encourage self-sufficiency. For example, under federal housing rules, minimum rents of up to $50 are typically charged to assisted tenants for whom 30 percent of income is less than that amount, but PHAs in San Diego and Portland, Oregon, have programs that increase those minimum rents over time for households that receive supportive services to help tenants increase their income.

[26] See Department of Housing and Urban Development, *Evaluation of the Family Self-Sufficiency Program: Prospective Study* (prepared by Abt Associates and Planmatics, February 2011), p. 25, www.huduser.org/portal/publications/ affhsg/eval_fssp.html. On average, upon enrollment, participants in the study had annual income that was 14 percent higher than that of the general FSS population, higher employment rates (69 percent compared with 51 percent), and higher educational attainment (75 percent had at least a high school diploma compared with 57 percent). For additional studies of changes in income for people in the FSS program, see Department of Housing and Urban Development, *Evaluation of the Self-Sufficiency Program: Retrospective Analysis, 1996 to 2000* (prepared by Westat, April 2004), www.huduser.org/portal/publications/econdev/selfsufficiency.html; Edgar O. Olsen and others, "The Effects of Different Types of Housing Assistance on Earnings and Employment," *Cityscape,* vol. 8, no. 2 (2005), pp. 163–187, www.huduser. org/periodicals/cityscpe/vol8num2/ ch8.pdf (267 KB); and Nandita Verma and others, *Working Toward Self-Sufficiency: Early Findings From a Program for Housing Voucher Recipients in New York City* (MDRC, December 2012), www.mdrc.org/ publication/working-toward-self-sufficiency.

[27] See MDRC, *The Family Self-Sufficiency Program Demonstration* (MDRC, 2012), www.mdrc.org/project/family-self-sufficiencyprogram-demonst ration#overview.

[28] The marginal tax rate is the percentage of an additional dollar of earnings that is paid in taxes or offset by reductions in benefits from government programs. For a detailed discussion of how increases in earnings can cause reductions in assistance provided through cash and in-kind benefits to people of reduced means, see Congressional Budget Office, *Effective*

Marginal Tax Rates for Low- and Moderate-Income Workers (November 2012), www.cbo.gov/publication/43709.

[29] See Brian A. Jacob and Jens Ludwig, "The Effects of Housing Assistance on Labor Supply: Evidence From a Voucher Lottery," *American Economic Review*, vol. 102, no. 1 (February 2012), pp. 272–304, www.aeaweb. org/articles.php?doi=10.1257/ aer.102.1.272. Although the data do not directly measure the number of hours worked, the only other explanations for reduced earnings would be that the decline in employment was concentrated among relatively high earners or that assisted residents shifted to jobs that paid less.

[30] See Michelle Wood and others, "Housing Affordability and Family Well-Being: Results From the Housing Voucher Evaluation," *Housing Policy Debate,* vol. 19, no. 2 (January 2008), pp. 367–412, http://dx.doi.org/ 10.1080/ 10511482.2008.9521639.

[31] See Deven Carlson and others, "Long-Term Earnings and Employment Effects of Housing Voucher Receipt," *Journal of Urban Economics*, vol. 71, no. 1 (January 2012), pp. 128–150, http://tinyurl.com/ndevvs2.

[32] The options discussed here do not apply to programs managed by the roughly 40 PHAs participating in the Moving to Work program. That program allows PHAs to seek exemption from most federal housing rules to reduce costs, increase efficiency, promote tenants' self-sufficiency, and increase housing choices. Participating PHAs can blend funding streams for different programs, experiment with rent and eligibility rules, and adhere to modified reporting requirements. Currently, 0.3 million households (representing about 6 percent of all directly subsidized units) are served by PHAs that participate in the program.

[33]. See Department of Housing and Urban Development, "Picture of Subsidized Households" (accessed July 29, 2015), www.huduser.org/ portal/datasets/picture/yearlydata.html.

[34] Those estimated increases in participation reflect CBO's judgment about whether households would know of the available assistance and whether the benefits of participating would outweigh the costs. Households, for example, might consider whether participation would require an increase in their out-of-pocket housing expenses, a move, or a shift in status from homeowner to renter. Property owners might consider how participation would influence their ability to maintain occupancy and receive timely compensation; they might also take into consideration the transaction costs of complying with the program's requirements, such as quality inspections.

[35] See Michael D. Eriksen and Amanda Ross, "Housing Vouchers and the Price of Rental Housing," *American Economic Journal: Economic Policy*, vol. 7, no. 3 (August 2015), pp. 154–176, http://tinyurl.com/oogjz57; C. Lance Barnett, "Expected and Actual Effects of Housing Allowances on Housing Prices," *Real Estate Economics*, vol. 7, no. 3 (September 1979), pp. 277–297, http://tinyurl.com/neapdts; and Raymond J. Struyk and Marc Bendick Jr., eds., *Housing Vouchers for the Poor: Lessons From a National Experiment* (Urban Institute Press, 1981).

[36] See Michael D. Eriksen and Amanda Ross, "Housing Vouchers and the Price of Rental Housing," *American Economic Journal: Economic Policy* , vol. 7, no. 3 (August 2015), pp. 154–176, http://tinyurl.com/oogjz57.

[37] See Scott Susin, "Rent Vouchers and the Price of Low-Income Housing," *Journal of Public Economics*, vol. 83, no. 1 (January 2002), pp. 109–152, http://dx.doi.org/10.1016/S0047-2727(01)00081-0; and Edgar O. Olsen, "Housing Programs for Low-Income Households," in Robert A. Moffitt, ed., *Means-Tested Transfer Programs in the United States* (University of Chicago Press, 2003), pp. 365–442, http://papers.nber.org/books/ moff03-1.

[38] See Department of Housing and Urban Development, *Capital Needs in the Public Housing Program* (prepared by Abt Associates, November 2010), http://go.usa.gov/3Frdz (PDF, 1.03 MB).

[39] A PHA can also pledge up to 100 percent of capital funds that it projects will be awarded to it solely for developing new public housing to replace units that have been demolished or sold—such funds are known as replacement housing factor grants. In total, however, a PHA cannot pledge more than 50 percent of its overall projected capital funding, which includes both the basic capital fund grants and any replacement housing factor grants. (PHAs may pledge more than one-third of the capital and replacement housing factor funds that they have received at the time their capital fund financing proposal was approved.) For program information, see Use of Capital Funds for Financing, 24 C.F.R. §905 Subpart E (2010).

[40] The first project was approved in November 2000. See Department of Housing and Urban Development, "Capital Fund Financing Program (CFFP): List of Transactions Approved to Date" (accessed July 29, 2015) http://go. usa.gov/3KWKJ.

[41] See Department of Housing and Urban Development, "Rental Assistance Demonstration (RAD), Program Information: Information on Applications, Reservations, and Waiting List" (accessed July 29, 2015), http://portal.hud.gov/hudportal/ HUD?src=/RAD/info.

[42]. PHAs have been allowed, since 1998, to consolidate operations while maintaining their own boards of directors. In July 2014, HUD proposed a rule to treat PHAs with consolidated operations as one agency for the purposes of financial reporting by and auditing of HCV programs. In addition, the Consolidated Appropriations Act, 2014, allows PHAs with consolidated operations to submit combined reports for public housing. See Government Accountability Office, *Housing Choice Vouchers: Options Exist to Increase Program Efficiencies*, GAO-12-300 (March 19, 2012), www.gao.gov/products/GAO-12-300; Department of Housing and Urban Development, Office of Policy, Program and Legislative Initiatives, *Rebalancing HUD's Oversight and Small PHAs' Regulatory Burdens* (prepared by IBM Business Consulting Services, 2008); Streamlining Requirements Applicable to Formation of Consortia by Public Housing Agencies, 79 Fed. Reg. 40019 (proposed July 11, 2014); and sec. 212 of the Consolidated Appropriations Act, 2014, P.L. 113-76.

[43] See Department of Housing and Urban Development, *Fiscal Year 2013 Budget: Justifications for Estimates* (2012), http://go.usa.gov/3KkDH, *FY 2014 Congressional Justifications* (2013), http://go.usa.gov/3KkW4, *FY 2015 Congressional Justifications* (2014), http://go.usa.gov/3KkZF, and *FY 2016 Congressional Justifications* (2015), http://go.usa.gov/3KkB3.

[44] See Government Accountability Office, *Housing Choice Vouchers: Options Exist to Increase Program Efficiencies*, GAO-12-300 (March 19, 2012), www.gao.gov/products/GAO-12-300.

[45] A recently released draft report by HUD explores the costs of administering the HCV program. See *Housing Choice Voucher Program Administrative Fee Study* (prepared by Abt Associates, April 2015), www.huduser.org/ portal/hcvfeestudy.html.

[46] See Robert A. Collinson and Peter Ganong, "The Incidence of Housing Voucher Generosity" (May 2015), http://dx.doi.org/ 10.2139/ssrn.2255 799.

[47] See Department of Housing and Urban Development, *Evaluation of the Mark-to-Market Program* (prepared by Econometrica and Abt Associates, August 2004), pp. ix, 27–28, 39–40, www.huduser.org/ portal/ publications/ PUBASST/ evalm2m.html.

[48] Robert Barrick, Department of Housing and Urban Development, personal communication (June 26, 2014). Data do not include Section 202 project-based housing for the elderly or Section 811 project-based housing for people with disabilities.

[49] See Department of Housing and Urban Development, *Evaluation of the Mark-to-Market Program* (prepared by Econometrica and Abt Associates, August 2004), pp. x, 27–28, 39–40, www.huduser.org/portal/publications/ PUBASST/ evalm2m.htm; sec. 514(g) of Multifamily Assisted Housing Reform and Affordability Act of 1997, P.L. 105-65, 111 Stat. 1384, 1395.

[50] Notice of Certain Operating Cost Adjustment Factors, 77 Fed. Reg. 63324 (October 16, 2012), 78 Fed. Reg. 56911 (September 16, 2013), 79 Fed. Reg. 59502 (October 2, 2014). Over the past few years, the average operating cost adjustment factor has been about 2 percent.

[51] See Department of Housing and Urban Development, *Section 8 Renewal Policy Guide* (May 18, 2012), http://go.usa.gov/3KBHG.

[52] See Department of Housing and Urban Development, "M2M Status Report" (April 13, 2015), http://go.usa.gov/3KBHz.

[53]. Housing Trust Fund Interim Rule, 80 Fed. Reg. 5199 (January 30, 2015).

[54] Revenue estimates, unlike estimates of tax expenditures, take into account the interaction between tax provisions and people's behavioral responses to a change in the tax code.

[55] See Joint Center for Housing Studies of Harvard University, *Long-Term Low Income Housing Tax Credit Policy Questions* (November 2010) http://tinyurl.com/mxa7ktm; Nathaniel Baum-Snow and Justin Marion, "The Effects of Low Income Housing Tax Credit Developments on Neighborhoods," *Journal of Public Economics*, vol. 93 (January 2009), pp. 654–666, http://tinyurl.com/ k2m7ldp; and "Diamonds in the Rough: The Best of Times and Worst of Times for Preservation Deals," *Tax Credit Advisor* (June 2012), http://tinyurl.com/k2dk5b7.

[56] See Ingrid Gould Ellen and others, "Does Federally Subsidized Rental Housing Depress Neighborhood Property Values?" *Journal of Policy Analysis and Management*, vol. 26, no. 2 (Spring 2007), pp. 257–280, http://dx.doi. org/10.1002/pam.20247.

[57] See Gregory S. Burge, "Do Tenants Capture the Benefits From the Low-Income Housing Tax Credit Program?" *Real Estate Economics*, vol. 39, no. 1, pp. 71–96 (Spring 2011), http://tinyurl.com/05bja93.

End Notes for Appendix

[1] Also, under authority provided in the Emergency Economic Stabilization Act of 2008 (Division A of Public Law 110-343), which established the Troubled Asset Relief Program (TARP), the Treasury will ultimately disburse $28 billion through several housing programs that help homeowners avoid foreclosure, CBO estimates. Although many of the programs' participants have low income, the programs do not specifically target that population. The programs are temporary, however, and therefore are not included in this appendix. See Congressional Budget Office, Report on the Troubled Asset Relief Program—March 2015 (March 2015), www.cbo.gov/publication/50034.

[2] Estimates of tax expenditures are based on people's behavior with the provisions in place and do not reflect how people would adjust their activities in response to changes in the tax code. Thus, the estimates do not reflect the amount of revenue that would be raised if those provisions were eliminated from the tax code.

[3] See Joint Committee on Taxation, Estimates of Federal Tax Expenditures for Fiscal Years 2014–2018, JCX-97-14 (August 2014), www.jct.gov/publications.html?func=select&id=5. All estimates in this appendix that are attributed to JCT are from this source.

[4] See Internal Revenue Service, "Instructions for Schedule A (Form 1040)" (January 5, 2015), www.irs.gov/pub/irs-pdf/www.irs.gov/pub/irs-pdf/ i1040sca.pdf (636 KB).

[5] See Congressional Budget Office, "Federal Programs that Guarantee Mortgages—Baseline Projections" (May 2013), www.cbo.gov/publication/43882. (The actual volume of the loan guarantees in 2014 was about $710 billion; see Fannie Mae, "Monthly Summary: Total Book of Business Components" [October 2014], Table 1, www.fanniemae. com/portal/about-us/ investor-relations/monthly-summary.html; and Freddie Mac, "Monthly Volume Summary: Total Mortgage Portfolio" [October 2014], Table 1, www.freddiemac.com/investors/volsum.) For a detailed explanation of the differences in how CBO and the Administration's Office of Management and Budget account for the activities of Fannie Mae and Freddie Mac in the budget, see Congressional Budget Office, Transitioning to Alternative Structures for Housing Finance (December 2014), pp. 14–15, www.cbo.gov/publication/49765.

[6] For an explanation of the fair-value approach, and how it compares with the way that federal credit programs and loan guarantees are accounted for in the budget, see Congressional Budget Office, Budgetary Estimates for the Single-Family Mortgage Guarantee Program of the Federal Housing Administration (September 2014), www.cbo.gov/publication/45740.

[7] Francesca Castelli and others, Modeling the Budgetary Costs of FHA's Single-Family Mortgage Insurance, Working Paper 2014-05 (Congressional Budget Office, September 2014), www.cbo.gov/ publication/45711; and Congressional Budget Office, Budgetary Estimates for the Single-Family Mortgage Guarantee Program of the Federal Housing Administration (September 2014), www.cbo.gov/ publication/45740.

[8] Census Bureau, "American Housing Survey, National Summary Tables—AHS 2013" (accessed July 29, 2014), Table C-14B-00, www.census.gov/programs-surveys/ ahs/data.html.

In: Federal Housing Assistance Programs ... ISBN: 978-1-63484-336-2
Editor: Eric Collier

Chapter 2

OVERVIEW OF FEDERAL HOUSING ASSISTANCE PROGRAMS AND POLICY*

Maggie McCarty, Libby Perl and Katie Jones

SUMMARY

The federal government has been involved in providing housing assistance to lower-income households since the 1930s. In the beginning, the federal government was involved in supporting the mortgage market (through establishment of the Federal Housing Administration (FHA) and the government-sponsored enterprises) and in promoting construction of low-rent public housing for lower-income families through local public housing authorities (PHAs). Over time, the role of the federal government has shifted away from providing construction-based subsidies to providing rental subsidies; private developers and property owners now play a larger role; and more federal funding has been provided to states and localities.

Today's federal housing assistance programs fall into three main categories: rental housing assistance, assistance to state and local governments, and assistance for homeowners. Most of these programs are administered by the Department of Housing and Urban Development (HUD). Current housing assistance programs include Section 8 vouchers and project-based rental assistance, public housing, housing for the

---

* This is an edited, reformatted and augmented version of a Congressional Research Service publication RL34591, prepared for Members and Committees of Congress, dated April 15, 2014.

elderly (Section 202), housing for persons with disabilities (Section 811), rural rental assistance (the United States Department of Agriculture's Section 521 program), Community Development Block Grants (CDBG), HOME Investment Partnerships Block Grants, Low-Income Housing Tax Credits (LIHTC), homeless assistance programs, FHA and Veterans' Administration mortgage insurance, and the mortgage interest deduction in the tax code.

Most of the federal housing assistance programs are aimed at making housing affordable for low-income families. Housing affordability—housing that costs no more than 30% of family income—is considered the largest housing problem today. Rental assistance programs, which are the largest source of direct housing assistance for low-income families, all allow families to pay affordable, income-based rents; however, different forms of assistance target different types of households, including the elderly, persons with disabilities, and families with children. Several trends in federal housing policy have emerged in recent decades. As the focus of federal housing assistance has shifted away from construction-based subsidies to rental assistance, block grants, and LIHTC, state and local governments have had greater access to federal resources to fund local housing and community development priorities. This shift in federal funding has also led affordable housing developers to pursue mixed financing: the use of multiple streams of federal funding, state, and local funding, or private financing. In the past, lagging homeownership rates among low-income and minority households have prompted several Presidents to promote homeownership-based housing policies. However, given the severe downturn in U.S. housing markets in recent years and the resulting high foreclosure rate, it is unclear to what degree federal policy will continue to focus on increasing access to homeownership.

INTRODUCTION

The federal government has played a role in subsidizing housing construction and providing homeownership and rental assistance for lower-income households since the 1930s. Today, Congress funds a number of programs to help meet the housing needs of poor and vulnerable populations. The programs are primarily administered by the Department of Housing and Urban Development (HUD), with some assistance provided to rural communities through the Department of Agriculture and some tax benefits administered through the Department of the Treasury. The modern housing assistance programs include both relatively flexible grants to state and local governments to serve homeless people, build affordable housing, provide assistance to first-time homebuyers, and promote community development and more structured, direct assistance programs that provide low-cost apartments and rental vouchers to poor families, administered through local public, quasi-public, and private intermediaries. The federal government also makes tax credits available to states to distribute to developers of low-cost housing and provides insurance to lenders that make mortgages to eligible homebuyers. The federal government's largest housing program, however, is arguably the mortgage interest deduction, which is not targeted to lower-income households, but is available to all homeowners who pay mortgage interest and itemize their deductions.

This report begins with an overview of the history and evolution of federal housing assistance policy, followed by a description of today's major federal housing assistance programs, and concludes with a discussion of issues and trends in federal housing assistance policy. It is an expanded version of the Federal Housing Assistance section originally prepared for the 2008 edition of the Committee on Ways and Means publication, "Background Material and Data on the Programs within the Jurisdiction of the Committee on Ways and Means" (informally known as the Green Book). This report does not track current legislation.

History and Evolution of Federal Housing Assistance Policy

The Beginning of Federal Housing Assistance: FHA and Public Housing

The federal government's first major housing policy was formulated in response to trouble in the mortgage market resulting from the Great Depression. Until the early 1930s, most mortgages were written for terms of three to five years and required borrowers to make payments only on an annual basis. At the end of the three- or five-year terms, the remaining loan balance had to be repaid or the mortgage had to be renegotiated. Another feature of the mortgage market was that lenders would only lend 40% to 50% of the value of the property, so borrowers had to have the cash to complete the transaction or find someone willing to finance the balance (or part of the balance) in a second mortgage. During the Great Depression, however, lenders were unable or unwilling to refinance many of the loans that became due.

When borrowers could not pay the loan balances, lenders foreclosed on the loans and took possession of the properties.

It was against this background that the Housing Act of 1934 (P.L. 73-479) was enacted. The broad objectives of the act were to (1) encourage lenders to invest in housing construction, and (2) to stimulate employment in the building industry. The act created the Federal Housing Administration (FHA). FHA insured lenders against losses on home modernization and home improvement loans, created the Mutual Mortgage Insurance Fund to fund the operation of the newly-created mortgage insurance programs, and established national mortgage associations to buy and sell mortgages.

The creation of FHA also institutionalized a revolutionary idea: 20-year mortgages on which a loan would be completely repaid at the end of its term. If borrowers defaulted, FHA insured that the lender would be fully repaid. Eventually, lenders began to make long-term mortgages without FHA insurance as long as borrowers made significant down payments. Over time, 25- and 30- year mortgages have become standard mortgage products.

As in the case of the mortgage finance market, the federal government initially became involved in the provision of rental housing assistance in response to the Great Depression. In the early 1930s, a housing division was added to President Franklin D. Roosevelt's Works Progress Administration (WPA) as a part of the effort to create jobs and spur economic growth.[1] The Housing Division acquired land and built multifamily housing projects for occupancy by lower-income families across the country. However, the Housing Division's activities proved controversial with local government officials who thought that they were not consulted in the process.

Against this backdrop, the U.S. Housing Act of 1937 (P.L. 75-412) was enacted. It replaced the WPA's Housing Division and its projects by establishing a new, federal United States Housing Agency (a precursor agency to today's Department of Housing and Urban Development) and a new Low-Rent Public Housing program. The new program required partnerships between the federal government, states, and localities. States that wished to receive assistance in building low-rent public housing were required to pass enabling legislation creating new, quasi-governmental, local public housing authorities (PHAs). These PHAs could then apply to the federal government for funding to aid in the construction and maintenance of low-rent housing developments targeted to low-income families. The act declared that it was the policy of the United States:

> to promote the general welfare of the nation by employing its funds and credit, as provided in this Act, to assist the several states and their political subdivisions to alleviate present and recurring unemployment and to remedy the unsafe and unsanitary housing conditions and the acute shortage of decent, safe, and sanitary dwellings for families of low-income, in rural or urban communities, that are injurious to the health, safety, and morals of the citizens of the nation.

Housing was a major issue in the presidential and congressional races during 1948. President Harry S. Truman's pledge to address the postwar housing shortage and the problem of urban slums played a key role in his margin of victory.[2] In his State of the Union Address in 1949 unveiling the "Fair Deal," President Truman observed that "Five million families are still living in slums and firetraps. Three million families share their homes with others."[3]

He further stated

> The housing shortage continues to be acute. As an immediate step, the Congress should enact the provisions for low-rent public housing, slum clearance, farm housing, and housing research which I have repeatedly recommended. The number of low-rent public housing units provided for in the legislation should be increased to 1 million units in the next 7 years. Even this number of units will not begin to meet our need for new housing.

The Housing Act of 1949 (P.L. 81-171) declared the goal of "a decent home and a suitable living environment for every American family." The act: (1) established a federal urban redevelopment and slum clearance program, authorizing federal loans of $1 billion over a five-year period to help local redevelopment agencies acquire slum properties and assemble sites for redevelopment; (2) reactivated the public housing program for low-income families (which had been on hold during World War II), authorizing subsidies to local housing authorities sufficient to build 810,000 units over six years; (3) expanded the FHA's mortgage insurance program to promote home building and homeownership; (4) created within the U.S. Department of Agriculture a program of financial assistance and subsidies to improve housing conditions on farms and in rural areas; and (5) authorized federal grants for research, primarily to improve the productivity of the housing industry.

Government Subsidization of Private Development

Through the 1950s, the federal government's role in housing assistance focused largely on public housing, which served a mostly poor population. Congress recognized that a gap existed in the market—few options existed for moderate income families whose incomes were too high to qualify for public housing, but too low to afford adequate market rate housing.[4] Proposals in Congress had been made to address the shortage of housing for moderate income households during the 1950s; however, no legislation had been enacted, in part due to the cost to the government of creating and funding a new program.[5] In order to avoid creating another large housing program with high expenditures, while at the same time finding a way to serve this segment of the population, Congress approved legislation at the end of the 1950s and throughout the 1960s that engaged the private sector in the development of affordable housing.

The Housing Act of 1959 (P.L. 86-372) was the first significant instance where government incentives were used to persuade private developers to build housing that would be affordable to low- and moderate-income households. As part of P.L. 86-372, Congress created the Section 202 Housing for the Elderly program. Through the Section 202 program, the federal government extended low-interest loans to private non-profit organizations for the development of affordable housing for moderate-income residents age 62 and older. The low interest rates were meant to ensure that units would be affordable, with non-profit developers able to charge lower rents and still have adequate revenue to pay back the government loans.

The Housing Act of 1961 (P.L. 87-70) further expanded the role of the private sector in providing housing to low- and moderate-income households. The act created the Section 221(d)(3) Below Market Interest Rate (BMIR) housing program, which both insured mortgages to private developers of multifamily housing and provided loans at low interest rates. The BMIR program expanded the pool of eligible borrowers to private for-profit developers and government entities, as well as non-profit developers. Eligible developers included cooperatives, limited dividend corporations, and state or local government agencies. Like the Section 202 program, the low interest rates in the BMIR program were meant to ensure that building owners could offer affordable rents to tenants.

In 1965, the Housing and Urban Development Act (P.L. 89-117) added rental assistance to the list of incentives for private multifamily housing developers that participated in the Section 221(d)(3) BMIR program. P.L. 89-

117 created the Rent Supplement program, which capped the rents charged to participating tenants at 20% of their incomes and paid building owners the difference between 20% of a tenant's income and fair market rent.

The Housing and Urban Development Act of 1965 also created the Section 23 leased housing program, the first program to provide rent subsidies for use in existing private rental market units. The same PHAs that administered the public housing program were authorized to enter into contracts with landlords in the private market. These contracts authorized payments to landlords who rented units to low-income tenants. Tenants paid one quarter of their income toward rent in these private units, and the federal subsidies made up the difference between the tenant payments and rent for the units.

In 1968, the Housing and Urban Development Act (P.L. 90-448) created the Section 236 and Section 235 programs. In the Section 236 program, the government subsidized private developers' mortgage interest payments so that they would not pay more than 1% toward interest. Like the low interest rate loans provided through the Section 221(d)(3) BMIR program, the Section 236 interest subsidies were meant to ensure that units would be affordable to low- and moderate-income tenants, although some units also received rent subsidies (referred to as Rental Assistance Payments (RAP)) to make them affordable to the lowest-income tenants. The Section 235 program instituted similar mortgage interest reduction payments for individual homeowners rather than multifamily housing developers.

Under the public housing program, tenants generally paid rent in an amount equal to the costs of operating the assisted housing in which they lived. Over time, as operating costs rose, there was a concern that the below-market rents being charged to families were too high to be affordable to the poorest families. The Brooke Amendment, which was included as part of the Housing and Urban Development Act of 1969 (P.L. 91-152), limited tenant contributions toward rent in all rent assisted units (including public housing and all project-based rental assistance units) to an amount equal to 25% of tenant income (this was later raised to 30%). The Brooke Amendment is considered responsible for codifying an income-based rent structure in federal housing programs.

By the end of the 1960s, subsidies to private developers had resulted in the creation of hundreds of thousands of housing units. Approximately 700,000 units of housing had been built through the Section 236 and Section 221(d)(3) programs alone.[6] The Section 202 program had created more than 45,000 units for elderly households.[7] The Section 235 and Section 23 leased-housing programs provided ownership and rental subsidies for thousands more. Through 1972, the Section 235 program subsidized nearly 400,000 homeowners,[8] while the Section 23 leased-housing program provided rent subsidies for more than 38,000 private market rental units.[9] Despite the growth in the role of private developers, public housing was still the largest housing subsidy program, with roughly a million units built and subsidized by the early 1970s.[10]

Rethinking the Strategy: From Construction Subsidies to Rent Subsidies

By the early 1970s, concern was growing about the cost, efficacy, and equity of the construction-based housing subsidy programs, such as the Section 236 and public housing programs. Then-President Richard M. Nixon criticized the existing programs as not equitably serving families in the same circumstances, providing poor quality housing, being too costly, and placing some families in homes they could not afford.[11] Out of these concerns, President Nixon declared a moratorium on all new activity under the major housing subsidy programs—except for the Section 23 leased-housing program—beginning in January 1973. Assisted housing activity slowly restarted in response to lawsuits and new legislation.

The Housing Act of 1974 (P.L. 93-383) was the first omnibus housing legislation since 1968 and the first such legislation following the Nixon moratorium. The act created a new low-income rental assistance program, referred to as Section 8. Although the 1960s had seen rental assistance programs like Rent Supplement and Section 23, the scale of the Section 8 program made it the first comprehensive rental assistance program. The Section 8 program combined features of the Section 236 program, which was popular with advocates of construction-based subsidies, and the Section 23 leased housing program, which used the existing housing stock and was popular with the Nixon Administration. Through Section 8, the federal government provided private property owners monthly assistance payments for new or substantially rehabilitated rental units. In exchange for monthly rental payments, property owners would agree to rent to eligible low-income families (defined as families with incomes at or below 80% of local area median income) who would pay an income-based rent. It also provided PHAs with the authority to enter into rental assistance contracts for existing, private market units.

Over time, the use of Section 8 in new construction and substantial rehabilitation projects was found to be more expensive than its use in existing housing. The Housing and Urban-Rural Recovery Act of 1983 (P.L. 98-181) repealed HUD's authority to enter into new Section 8 contracts tied to new construction and substantial rehabilitation, but retained HUD's authority to issue new contracts for existing properties. The act also created a new demonstration program to test a modified use of Section 8, referred to as vouchers. Vouchers were similar to the use of Section 8 rent subsidies in existing housing, but provided more flexibility to PHAs, particularly by permitting families to pay more than 30% of their incomes in rent. The demonstration was made permanent in 1985.

Increasing Role of State and Local Governments

By the mid-1980s, federal housing programs had gone through a number of iterations. Some programs had been scrapped as inefficient, subject to fraud and abuse, or too expensive. Shifting federal priorities—towards reducing taxes and increasing military spending in response to the Cold War—reduced funding available for social programs, including housing assistance. Creation of assisted housing with federal funds was on the decline, with production between 1982 and 1988 slowing significantly.[12] In addition, existing affordable rental units were being lost as use restrictions between private owners and HUD expired or owners chose to prepay their low-interest mortgages and begin charging market-rate rent.[13]

As a result of reduced federal support for housing, state and local governments and private for- or non-profit organizations began to take the initiative in developing innovative ways of providing housing in their communities.[14] Policy makers acknowledged that, in some cases, local communities had better knowledge about how to provide housing than the federal government, and might be able to provide housing more efficiently than HUD.[15] From the late 1980s through the 1990s, Congress acknowledged the value of local control and gave more decision-making authority over housing policy to state and local governments through the creation of block grants and tax credits.

In 1986, the Low Income Housing Tax Credit (LIHTC) program was created as part of the Tax Reform Act of 1986 (P.L. 99-514). The LIHTC was not initially part of the bill that became the Tax Reform Act (H.R. 3838). However, because portions of H.R. 3838 eliminated the favorable treatment of real estate investment income, Members added the LIHTC program to the bill in order to ensure that developers would have an incentive to continue to construct low- and moderate-income housing.[16]

The LIHTC program, intentionally or not, was one of the first major programs to give a good deal of control over housing policy to states and localities. Tax credits are allocated to states based on population. States then have discretion in setting priorities as to how the credits will be used. While states must prioritize projects that serve the lowest income tenants for the longest period of time, they may choose to allocate credits based on criteria such as the tenant populations served— those with special needs, families with children, or those on public housing waiting lists.

In 1990, Congress created another large, flexible block grant to states and localities. The National Affordable Housing Act of 1990 (NAHA, P.L. 101-625) authorized the HOME Investment Partnerships program. HOME was modeled after an earlier block grant, the Community Development Block Grant (CDBG), which was created as part of the Housing Act of 1974 to consolidate several special purpose grants funding many activities other than housing, such as neighborhood revitalization, open space, and water and sewer grants. NAHA directed that HOME funds be allocated to states and localities based on a formula and that funds be targeted to assist families with incomes at or below 60% of area median income. Recipient jurisdictions were permitted to use funds to assist homeowners, construct rental housing, or provide rental assistance, and they were required to establish plans for spending their funds, meet match requirements, and partner with local non-profits.

The Native American Housing Assistance and Self-Determination Act of 1996 (NAHASDA, P.L. 104-330), reorganized the system of federal housing assistance to Native Americans by eliminating several separate programs of assistance and replacing them with a single block grant program. In addition to simplifying the process of providing housing assistance, the purpose of NAHASDA was to provide federal assistance for Indian tribes in a manner that recognizes the right of Indian self-determination and tribal self-governance.

Reforming Rental Assistance

Throughout the 1990s, concern about the state of public housing grew. The public perceived public housing as mismanaged, of poor quality, and dangerous.[17] At the same time, interest was growing in reforming social programs by devolving control to the states and increasing their focus on promoting work and self-sufficiency. Concern over the state of public housing—and the influence of the 1996 welfare reform debate and legislation—led to proposals for major public and assisted housing reforms. Several years of debate in Congress culminated with the enactment of the Quality Housing and Work Opportunity Reconciliation Act of 1998 (P.L. 105-276).

The purposes of QHWRA, as defined in the act, were to deregulate PHAs; provide more flexible use of federal assistance to PHAs; facilitate mixed income communities; decrease concentrations of poverty in public housing; increase accountability and reward effective management of PHAs; create incentives and economic opportunities for residents assisted by PHAs to work and become self-sufficient; consolidate the Section 8 voucher and certificate programs into a single market-driven program; remedy the problems of troubled PHAs; and replace or revitalize severely distressed public housing projects.

Specific reforms in QHWRA included increased income targeting in the voucher program, removal of federal preference categories for housing assistance, enactment of a limited community service requirement in public housing, creation of the Section 8 Housing Choice Voucher program (a hybrid of the Section 8 voucher and certificate programs), authorization of the HOPE VI program (which had been in place, but unauthorized since the early 1990s), consolidation and reform of funding for public housing, and modifications to the assessment systems for PHAs.

TODAY'S HOUSING ASSISTANCE PROGRAMS

Today's system for providing housing assistance to low-income families is made up of programs that fall into three main categories: rental housing assistance, federal assistance to state and local governments, and homeownership assistance. Rental assistance is provided primarily through rent vouchers that families can use in the private market, below-market rental units owned by PHAs or private landlords under contract with the federal government, and, to a limited extent, construction of new below-market rental units. Assistance to state and local governments comes in a number of forms, including broad flexible block grants that can be used for rental, homeownership, or community development purposes, special purpose block grants, and programs based in the tax system. Homeownership assistance includes direct assistance to defray homebuying costs, as well as mortgage insurance programs to help provide incentives for the private market to meet the needs of underserved segments of the population.

The following section provides a description of the major housing assistance programs that fall into these three categories.

Rental Housing Assistance

Section 8 Vouchers

Section 8 vouchers are a form of tenant-based rental assistance funded by the federal government, administered locally by quasi-governmental public housing authorities (PHAs) and provided to private landlords on behalf of low-income families. (The program is codified at 42 U.S.C. §1437f(o)). Generally, eligible families with vouchers live in the housing of their choice in the private market and the voucher pays the difference between the family's contribution toward rent and the actual rent for the unit. Specifically, a family pays 30% of its adjusted income toward rent (although they can choose to pay more) and the PHA, which receives funding from HUD, makes payments to the landlord based on a maximum subsidy set by the PHA (based on the local fair market rent established by HUD), less the tenant's contribution. Families are eligible to receive a voucher if they are very low-income (earning 50% or less of the local area median income) or low-income (earning 80% or less of the local area median income) but meet other special criteria (for example, are elderly or have disabilities). However, PHAs must provide 75% of all vouchers available in a year to extremely low-income families (earning 30% or less of the area median income). Vouchers are nationally portable; once a family receives a voucher, it can take that voucher and move to any part of the country where a voucher program is being administered.

There are several special forms of Section 8 vouchers. Tenant protection vouchers are provided to families who would otherwise be displaced from other HUD programs. Some tenant protection vouchers, called enhanced vouchers, can have higher values than regular vouchers. PHAs also have the discretion to "project-base" some of their vouchers. Project-based vouchers are attached to specific housing units rather than given to families to use in the homes of their choosing. Another special form of voucher is the homeownership voucher; PHAs have the discretion to allow eligible first-time homebuyers to use their vouchers to make monthly mortgage payments.

The voucher program is not an entitlement program. Families that wish to receive a voucher must generally apply to their local PHA and are placed on a waiting list, the length of which varies by community and can range from several months to many years. Congress has authorized and funded roughly 2 million vouchers. The funding for those vouchers is provided annually by Congress in the appropriations for HUD. The Section 8 voucher program is the largest of HUD's rental assistance programs, serving the largest number of households and accounting, in recent years, for more than one-third of the Department's budget. Congress has generally renewed all existing vouchers each year; in some years, Congress also creates new vouchers to serve additional families, referred to as incremental vouchers. The current distribution of vouchers across PHAs results from a variety of allocation methods used in the past: formula-based, competitive, and other. While the distribution of funding to PHAs is generally based on the number of vouchers that they have and the cost of those vouchers, the exact distribution formula has often been modified by Congress in the appropriations process.

Project-Based Section 8 Rental Assistance

Under the Section 8 project-based rental assistance program, HUD entered into contracts with private property owners under which owners agreed to rent their housing units to eligible low-income tenants for an income-based rent, and HUD agreed to pay the difference between tenants' contributions and a rent set by HUD. Families are eligible to live in project-based Section 8 units if they are low-income (having income at or below 80% of the area median income), but 40% of units made available each year must be reserved for extremely low-income families (those with income at or below 30% of the area median income).

No new project-based Section 8 contracts have been awarded since the mid-1980s, although existing contracts can be renewed upon their expiration. Roughly 1 million project-based units are still under contract and receive assistance. The original contracts were for 10-40 year periods and were provided with multi-year funding from Congress for the length of the contracts. Therefore, each year Congress only has to provide new funding for those contracts that have expired and require annual renewal (although, eventually, all of those long-term contracts will expire so all contracts will require annual funding). (See *Table 1* for appropriations information.) Not all contracts are renewed, so there has been a loss of project-based Section 8 units over time. When owners do not renew, tenants are provided with Section 8 tenant protection vouchers.

Public Housing

Low-rent public housing developments are owned and operated by local public housing authorities (PHAs) and subsidized and regulated by the federal government. (The program is codified at 42 U.S.C. §1437.) Generally, families are eligible to live in public housing if they are low-income (those with income at or below 80% of area median income), but 40% of public housing units that become available in a year must be given to extremely low-income families (those with income at or below 30% of area median income). As in the Section 8 voucher program, families living in public housing pay 30% of their adjusted income toward rent.

PHAs receive several streams of funding from HUD to help make up the difference between what tenants pay in rent and what it costs to maintain public housing. PHAs receive operating funds and capital funds through a formula allocation process; operating funds are used for management, administration, and the day-to-day costs of running a housing development and capital funds are used for modernization needs (such as replacing a roof or heating and cooling system, or reconfiguring units). PHAs can also apply for competitive HOPE VI—now Choice Neighborhoods—revitalization grants, which are used to demolish and rebuild, or substantially rehabilitate, severely distressed public housing, replacing it with mixed-income housing.

There are roughly 1.2 million public housing units under contract with the federal government, making public housing the second largest direct housing assistance program. The 1998 Public Housing Reform Act (P.L. 105-276) prohibited public housing authorities from increasing the total number of public housing units in their inventory; however, the number of public housing units had begun to steadily decline before then for a number of reasons. PHAs are authorized to demolish or sell their public housing developments with HUD's permission, and since the mid-1990s, they have not been required to replace those units with new units (although they must provide displaced families with Section 8 vouchers). The 1998 Act also provided authority to allow, and in some cases require, PHAs to convert their public housing units to vouchers. Also, the HOPE VI program has contributed to the demolition of more units than it has replaced.

Table 1. Appropriations for Section 8, FY2003-FY2013 ($ in millions)

Fiscal Year	Tenant-Based Section 8 Vouchers	Project-Based Section 8 Rental Assistance	Total Section 8
2003	—[a]	—[a]	17,116
2004	—[a]	—[a]	19,257
2005	14,766	5,298	20,064
2006	15,418[b]	5,037	20,455
2007	15,920	5,976	21,896
2008	15,703[c]	6,382	22,085
2009	16,225[d]	9,100[e]	25,325e
2010	18,184	8,558	26,741
2011	18,371	9,257	27,628
2012	18,264[f]	9,340	27,604
2013	17,964	8,851	26,815

Source: HUD Congressional Budget Justifications from FY2005 through FY2015. Enacted funding figures are taken from subsequent years' justifications. FY2013 funding levels reflect sequestration.

Note: Figures are not adjusted for rescissions of unobligated budget authority. Figures shown represent budget authority available in the fiscal year, not budget authority provided (which accounts for differences in advance appropriations from year to year).

a Prior to FY2005, Congress funded the Section 8 voucher and project-based rental assistance programs jointly.

b FY2006 figures for tenant-based rental assistance do not include $390 million in emergency appropriations for hurricane relief.

c Figure for tenant-based rental assistance is adjusted for $723 million rescission of current year budget authority enacted in FY2008.

d Figure for tenant-based rental assistance is adjusted for $750 million rescission of current year budget authority enacted in FY2009.

e Includes a $2 billion supplemental appropriation provided under the American Recovery and Reinvestment Act (P.L. 111-5). Does not include a $250 million supplemental appropriation for green energy retrofits appropriated under this account by P.L. 111-5.

f Figure for tenant-based rental assistance is adjusted for $650 million rescission of current year budget authority enacted in FY2012.

Table 2. Appropriations for Public Housing, FY2003-FY2013 ($ in millions)

Fiscal Year	Operating Fund	Capital Fund	HOPE VI/Choice Neighborhoods	Total Public Housing
2003	3,577	2,712	570	6,859
2004	3,579	2,696	149	6,424
2005	2,438	2,579	143	5,160
2006	3,564	2,439	99	6,102
2007	3,864	2,439	99	6,402
2008	4,200	2,439	100	6,739
2009	4,455	6,450[a]	120	11,025[a]
2010	4,775	2,500	200	7,475
2011	4,617	2,040	100	6,757
2012	3,962	1,875	120	5,957
2013	4,054	1,777	114	5,945

Source: HUD Congressional Budget Justifications from FY2005 through FY2015. Enacted funding figures are taken from subsequent years' justifications. FY2013 funding levels reflect sequestration.

Note: An accounting change enacted by Congress led to a one-time savings in the public housing operating fund in FY2005.

[a] Includes a $4 billion supplemental appropriation provided under the American Recovery and Reinvestment Act (P.L. 111-5).

Section 202 Supportive Housing for the Elderly Program and the Section 811 Housing for Persons with Disabilities Program

Through the Section 202 Supportive Housing for the Elderly program, HUD provides funds to nonprofit organizations which in turn build rental properties for low-income elderly households (those where one or more persons are age 62 or older). The program was created as part of the Housing Act of 1959 (P.L. 86-372). (The program is codified at 12 U.S.C. §1701q.) Section 202 is the only federal housing program that funds housing exclusively for elderly persons, although from approximately 1964 to 1990, non-elderly disabled households were eligible for residency in Section 202 properties.[18] Although the Section 202 program initially provided low-interest loans to nonprofit developers, since the early 1990s, the program has provided nonprofit developers with capital grants, together with project rental assistance contracts (rental assistance that is similar to project-based Section 8). Since FY2011, Congress has not appropriated funds for new capital grants. The current version of the Section 202 program serves very low-income elderly households (those with incomes at or below 50% of area median income).

The Section 811 Supportive Housing for Persons with Disabilities Program was created in 1990 as part of the Cranston-Gonzalez Affordable Housing Act (P.L. 101-625). (The program is codified at 42 U.S.C. §8013.)

Until the enactment of Section 811, the Section 202 program provided housing for persons with disabilities. Through Section 811, HUD provides capital grants to non-profit organizations to create rental housing that is affordable to very low-income households with an adult who has a disability.[19] The program also funds project rental assistance contracts to subsidize the rent paid by tenants. Housing built with capital grants may include group homes, independent living facilities, multifamily rental units, condominium units, and cooperative housing. Section 811 developers must provide supportive services to those residing in the units. In addition, through FY2010 the Section 811 program created tenant-based rental assistance, sometimes called "mainstream vouchers," that tenants can use to find housing in the private market, much like Section 8 vouchers. However, based on a law enacted in 2010 (P.L. 111-374), since FY2011, Section 811 tenant-based assistance has been funded via the Section 8 account. Also as part of P.L. 111-374, Section 811 rental assistance funds were made available to be used in conjunction with capital funding from other sources (such as Low Income Housing Tax Credits and HOME funds).

Other Rent-Restricted Units

The Section 236 program was a HUD initiative to encourage private developers to create housing affordable to low- and moderate-income households. The program, created as part of the Housing and Urban Development Act of 1968 (P.L. 90-448) was active in promoting new development from approximately 1969 to 1973.

(The program is codified at 12 U.S.C. §1715z-1.) The Section 236 program provided mortgage insurance to housing developers for the construction and rehabilitation of rental housing and continues to provide mortgage subsidies to building owners through a mechanism called Interest Reduction Payments (IRPs). IRPs are subsidies to owners that ensure that the owners will only pay 1% interest on their mortgages. Given the reduced financing costs, owners can charge below-market rents for Section 236 units. Many units also receive rental assistance payments through the Section 8 project-based rental assistance program, Rent Supplement program, or the

Rental Assistance Payments (RAP) program, making the units affordable to very low-income and extremely low-income families.

Table 3.Appropriations for Section 202 and Section 811, FY2003-FY2013 ($ in millions)

Fiscal Year	Section 202[a]	Section 811
2003	678	249
2004	698	249
2005	648	238
2006	635	231
2007	639	236
2008	629	237
2009	625	250
2010	668	300
2011	306	150[a]
2012	283	165[a]
2013	265	156[a]

Source: HUD Budget Justifications from FY2005 through FY2015. Enacted funding figures are taken from subsequent years' justifications. FY2013 funding levels reflect sequestration.

The amounts appropriated for Section 202 include funds for new capital grants, new project rental assistance, and renewals of or amendments to project rental assistance contracts. These figures do not include funds for Service Coordinators or the Assisted Living Conversion Program.

[a] Beginning in FY2011, appropriations for Section 811 vouchers were provided through the Section 8 tenant-based rental assistance account. In FY2011, appropriations were split between the Section 811 and Section 8 account. Thereafter, all funding has been provided through the Section 8 account.

The Section 221(d)(3) Below Market Interest Rate (BMIR) program was another HUD program that encouraged private developers to create affordable housing by offering FHA-insured loans with interest rates of 3%. The program was enacted as part of the Housing Act of 1961 (P.L. 87- 70) and actively insured new loans until 1968, when the Section 236 program replaced it as a vehicle for affordable housing development. (The Section 221(d)(3) program is codified at 12 U.S.C. §1715*l*.) Like Section 236, units created under this program are offered for below-market rents and units may also receive rental assistance.

Rural Rental Assistance (Section 521)

Title V of the Housing Act of 1949 authorized the U.S. Department of Agriculture (USDA) to make loans to farmers to enable them to construct, improve, repair, or replace dwellings and other farm buildings to provide decent, safe, and sanitary living conditions for themselves, their tenants, lessees, sharecroppers, and laborers. USDA was authorized to make grants, or combinations of loans and grants to those farmers who could not qualify to repay the full amount of a loan, but who needed the funds to make their dwellings sanitary or to remove health hazards to the occupants or the community. Although the act was initially targeted to farmers, over time the act has been amended to enable USDA to make housing loans and grants to rural residents in general.

The USDA housing programs are generally referred to by the section number under which they are authorized in the Housing Act of 1949, as amended. Under the Section 515 program, the Rural Housing Service of the USDA is authorized to make direct loans for the construction of rural rental and cooperative housing. (The Section 515 program is codified at 42 U.S.C. §1485.) The loans are made at a 1% interest rate and are repayable in 50 years. Except for public agencies, all borrowers must demonstrate that financial assistance from other sources is not enough to enable the borrower to provide the housing at terms that are affordable to the target population. USDA also provides guarantees on loans made by private lenders to developers of affordable rural rental housing for low- and moderate-income households under the Section 538 program. (The Section 538 program is codified at 42 U.S.C. §1490p-2.)

Under the Section 521 program, rental assistance payments, which are made directly to owners of rental properties, make up the difference between the tenants' rent payments and the USDA-approved rent for the Section 515 units. (The Section 521 program is codified at 42 U.S.C. §1490a.) Owners must agree to operate the property on a limited profit or nonprofit basis.

Funding for States and Localities

Low Income Housing Tax Credit

The LIHTC was enacted as part of the Tax Reform Act of 1986 (P.L. 99-514) and provides incentives for the development of affordable rental housing through federal tax credits administered through the Internal Revenue Service. (The program is codified at 26 U.S.C. §42.)

Table 4. Appropriations for USDA Section 521 Rental Assistance, FY2003-FY2013 ($ in millions)

Fiscal Year	Section 521 Rental Assistance
2003	724
2004	581
2005	587
2006	647
2007	616
2008	479
2009	903
2010	980
2011	954
2012	905
2013	837

Source: USDA Annual Budget Summaries from FY2005 through FY2015. Enacted funding figures are taken from subsequent years' budget summaries. FY2013 funding levels reflect sequestration.

The tax credits are disbursed to state housing finance agencies (HFAs) based on population. HFAs, in turn, award the credits to housing developers that agree to build or rehabilitate housing where a certain percentage of units will be affordable to low income households. Housing developers then sell the credits to investors and use the proceeds from sale of the credits to help finance the housing developments. The benefit of the tax credits to the purchasing investors is that they reduce the investor's federal income tax liability annually over a ten year period.

Because tax credits reduce the amount of private financing required to build or rehabilitate housing, the owners of developments financed through tax credits are able to charge lower rents. In order to qualify for the tax credits, at least 20% of units in a development must be occupied by households with incomes at or below 50% of area median income, or at least 40% of units must be occupied by households with incomes at or below 60% of area median income. Rent charged for the rent restricted units in a development may not exceed 30% of an imputed income limitation—calculated based on area median incomes. Units financed with tax credits must remain affordable for at least 15 years. As of 2011, more than 2.3 million units had been placed in service using

LIHTCs.[20] In FY2013, the Joint Committee on Taxation estimated that the LIHTC would result in a $6.4 billion tax expenditure.[21]

Mortgage Revenue Bonds

The federal government authorizes state and local governments to issue private activity bonds, up to a certain limit, which are exempt from federal taxes. One form of a private activity bond is a mortgage revenue bond (MRB). (MRBs are codified at 26 U.S.C. §143.) State or local governments—or their authorized agencies, such as housing finance agencics—sell MRBs to investors. Because the interest earned by bondholders is exempt from federal (and sometimes state) taxation, the bonds can be marketed at lower interest rates than would be required for similar taxable instruments. The proceeds of the bond sale, less issuance costs and reserves, are used to finance home mortgages to eligible (generally first-time) homebuyers. In effect, the tax exemption on the bonds provides an interest rate subsidy to homebuyers.

In order to qualify for the benefit, a borrower must not have been a homeowner in the past three years, the mortgage must be for the principal residence of the borrower, the purchase price may not exceed 90% (110% in targeted areas) of the average purchase price in the area, and the income of the borrower may not exceed 110% (140% in targeted areas) of the median income for the area. In FY2013, the Joint Committee on Taxation estimated that MRBs would result in a $1 billion tax expenditure.[22]

Community Development Block Grants

The Community Development Block Grant (CDBG) program was enacted as part of the Housing and Community Development Act of 1974 (P.L. 93-383), and is administered by HUD. (The program is codified at 42 U.S.C. §§5301-5321.)

The purpose of the CDBG program is to develop viable urban communities by providing decent housing, a suitable living environment, and expanding economic opportunities primarily for low- and moderate-income persons. The CDBG program distributes 70% of total funds through formula grants to entitlement communities—central cities of metropolitan areas, cities with populations of 50,000 or more, and urban counties—and the remaining 30% goes to states for use in small, non-entitlement communities.

Recipient communities may use CDBG funds for a variety of activities, although at least 70% of funds must be used to benefit low- and moderate-income persons. Eligible activities include the acquisition and rehabilitation of property for purposes such as public works, urban beautification, historic preservation; the demolition of blighted properties; services such as crime prevention, child care, drug abuse counseling, education, or recreation; neighborhood economic development projects; and the rehabilitation or development of housing as well as housing counseling services. In addition to its annual appropriations, Congress also has used the program's framework to provide additional, supplemental, and special appropriations to assist states and communities in responding to various economic crises and manmade and natural disasters.

HOME Block Grants

The HOME Investment Partnerships Program is a housing block grant program administered by HUD and designed to expand the supply of decent, safe, sanitary, and affordable housing. (The program is codified at 42 U.S.C. §§12741 et seq.) HOME funds are allocated via formula: 60% of funds are awarded to "participating jurisdictions" (localities which have populations above a certain threshold) and 40% are awarded to states to use in areas not served by participating jurisdictions. HOME grantees must match 25% of their HOME grants (with some exceptions) and submit a plan to HUD detailing their community housing needs and priorities.

HOME funds can be used for four main purposes: rehabilitation of owner-occupied housing, homebuyer assistance, rental housing construction and rehabilitation, and the provision of tenant-based rental assistance.

All HOME funds must be used to benefit low-income families (those with incomes at or below 80% of the area median income), and at least 90% of funds used for rental housing activities or tenant-based rental assistance must be used to benefit families with incomes at or below 60% of area median income.

Table 5. Appropriations for the Community Development Fund and CDBG, mFY2003-FY2013 ($ in millions)

Fiscal Year	CDBG Formula Grants[a]	Set-Asides	Community Development Fund Account Total
2003	4,340	565	4,905
2004	4,331	603	4,934
2005	4,117	585	4,702
2006	3,711	467	4,178
2007	3,711	61	3,772

Fiscal Year	CDBG Formula Grants[a]	Set-Asides	Community Development Fund Account Total
2008	3,593[b]	273	3,866
2009	4,642[c]	258	4,900
2010	3,950[d]	500	4,450
2011	3,303	198	3,501
2012	2,948	60	3,008
2013	3,078	57	3,135

Source: HUD Congressional Budget Justifications from FY2005 through FY2015. Enacted funding figures are taken from subsequent years' justifications. FY2013 funding levels reflect sequestration.

Note: The CDBG program is funded in an account called the Community Development Fund. That account also funds set-asides including funding for Economic Development Initiatives and Neighborhood Initiatives. This table excludes emergency funding provided to CDBG in response to disasters.

[a] Includes funding for insular areas.

[b] Does not include $4 billion provided in the CDF account for the Neighborhood Stabilization Program (NSP).

[c] Includes $1 billion in additional CDBG funding provided by P.L. 111-5. Does not include $2 billion provided in the CDF account for the Neighborhood Stabilization Program by P.L. 111-5.

[d] Does not include $1 billion provided in the CDF account for the Neighborhood Stabilization Program by P.L. 111-203.

Homeless Assistance Grants

The Homeless Assistance Grants were established in 1987 as part of the Stewart B. McKinney Homeless Assistance Act (P.L. 100-77). The grants, administered by HUD, fund housing and services for homeless persons. The Homeless Assistance Grants have gone through several permutations since their enactment, with the most recent change taking place when the grants were reauthorized in the 111th Congress by the Homeless Emergency Assistance and Rapid Transition to Housing (HEARTH) Act, enacted as part of the Helping Families Save Their Homes Act (P.L. 111-22).

Until enactment of the HEARTH Act, the Homeless Assistance Grants were made up of four programs: the Emergency Shelter Grants (ESG) program, the Supportive Housing Program (SHP), the Section 8 Moderate Rehabilitation Assistance for Single-Room Occupancy Dwellings (SRO) program, and the Shelter Plus Care (S+C) program.

Table 6. Appropriations for HOME, FY2003-FY2013 ($ in millions)

Fiscal Year	HOME Formula Grants	Set-Asides	HOME Account Total
2003	1,850	137	1,987
2004	1,855	150	2,006
2005	1,785	115	1,900
2006	1,677	81	1,757
2007	1,677	81	1,757
2008	1,625	79	1,704
2009	1,805	20	1,825[a]
2010	1,803	22	1,825
2011	1,587	19	1,607
2012	998	2	1,000
2013	946	2	948

Source: HUD Congressional Budget Justifications from FY2005 through FY2015. Enacted funding figures are taken from subsequent years' justifications. FY2013 funding levels reflect sequestration.

Note: In addition to funding HOME block grants, the HOME account also funds certain set-asides that have varied over the years. Such set-asides have included HOME funding for insular areas as well as programs such as the American Dream Downpayment Initiative (ADDI) and the Housing Counseling Assistance Program, among other things. ADDI, which provided funding for down payment and closing cost assistance for eligible first time homebuyers, was funded through the HOME account from FY2003-FY2008; Congress has not provided funding for ADDI in subsequent fiscal years. The Housing Counseling Assistance Program was funded through a set-aside in the HOME account until FY2009. Since that time, housing counseling has been funded in its own account rather than as a set-aside within the HOME account.

[a] Does not include $2 billion appropriated in this account for the Tax Credit Assistance Program by P.L. 111- 5.

The HEARTH Act maintained the ESG program, but renamed it the Emergency Solutions Grants program, and consolidated the three remaining programs (SHP, SRO, and S+C), sometimes referred to as the "competitive grants," into one program called the "Continuum of Care" (CoC) program. Funds appropriated for the ESG program continue to be distributed via formula to states and localities while funds for the CoC program, like its three predecessor programs, are distributed through a competition. Further, rural communities may apply separately for funds that otherwise would have been awarded as part of the Continuum of Care program through the Rural Housing Stability (RHS) grant program.

ESG program funds may be used by grantees in two categories: (1) emergency shelter and related services and (2) homelessness prevention and rapid rehousing. The statute limits use of funds in the first category to the greater of 60% of a state or local government's ESG allocation or the amount the recipient spent for these purposes in the year prior to the effective date of the HEARTH Act. CoC program funds may be used for transitional housing, permanent supportive housing, rapid rehousing, supportive services, and Homeless Management Information Systems. Grantees under the RHS program may use funds to assist people who are experiencing homelessness in many of the same ways as the CoC program. These include transitional housing, permanent housing, rapid rehousing, data collection, and a range of supportive services. Funds may also be used for homelessness prevention activities, relocation assistance, short-term emergency housing, and home repairs that are necessary to make housing habitable.

Housing Opportunities for Persons with AIDS

The Housing Opportunities for Persons with AIDS (HOPWA) program is the only federal program that provides funding specifically for housing for persons with acquired immunodeficiency syndrome (AIDS) and related illnesses. Congress established the HOPWA program as part of the National Affordable Housing Act (P.L. 101-625) in 1990. (The program is codified at 42 U.S.C. §§12901-12912.) HOPWA program funding is distributed both by formula allocations and competitive grants. HUD awards 90% of appropriated funds by formula to states and eligible metropolitan statistical areas (MSAs) that meet thresholds regarding population, AIDS cases, and AIDS incidence. Recipient states and MSAs may allocate grants to nonprofit organizations or administer the funds through government agencies. HOPWA grantees may use funds for a wide range of housing, social services, program planning, and development costs.

NAHASDA

The Native American Housing Assistance and Self-Determination Act of 1996 (NAHASDA, P.L. 104-330), reorganized the system of federal housing assistance to Native Americans by separating Native American programs from the public housing program, and by eliminating several separate programs of assistance and replacing them with a single block grant program.

Table 7. Appropriations for the Homeless Assistance Grants and HOPWA, FY2003-FY2013 ($ in millions)

Fiscal Year	Homeless Assistance Grants	HOPWA
2003	1,217	290
2004	1,260	295
2005	1,229	282
2006	1,327	286
2007	1,442	286
2008	1,586	300
2009	1,677	310
2010	1,865	335
2011	1,901	334
2012	1,901	332
2013	1,933	315

Source: HUD Budget Justifications from FY2005 through FY2015. Enacted funding figures are taken from subsequent years' justifications. FY2013 funding levels reflect sequestration.

Note: Funding for FY2009 Homeless Assistance Grants does not include $1.5 billion for the Homelessness Prevention and Rapid Re-Housing Program (HPRP) provided by P.L. 111-5.

In addition to simplifying the process of providing housing assistance, the purpose of NAHASDA was to provide federal assistance for Indian tribes in a manner that recognizes the right of Indian self-determination and tribal self-governance.

The act provides block grants to Indian tribes or their tribally designated housing entities (TDHEs) to use for a wide range of affordable housing activities through the Native American Housing Block Grant (NAHBG) program. The tribe must submit an Indian housing plan (IHP), which is reviewed by HUD for compliance with statutory and regulatory requirements. Funding is provided under a needs-based formula, which was developed pursuant to negotiated rule-making between tribal representatives and HUD. Tribes and TDHEs can leverage funds, within certain limits, by using future grants as collateral to obtain private loans for affordable housing activities under a guaranteed loan program, the Title VI Loan Guarantee Program.

Homeownership Assistance

Federal Housing Administration

The Federal Housing Administration (FHA) was established by the National Housing Act of 1934 (P.L. 73-479). Today an agency within HUD, FHA insures private lenders against losses on certain home mortgages. Since lenders are insured against loss if borrowers default, they are willing to make loans to borrowers who might not otherwise be served by the private market, particularly those with low down payments or little credit history. FHA-insured borrowers pay insurance premiums to FHA and are subject to limits on the size of loan that they can obtain.

Table 8. Appropriations for Native American Housing Block Grants, FY2003-FY2013 ($ in millions)

Fiscal Year	NAHASDA
2003	645
2004	650
2005	622
2006	624
2007	624
2008	624
2009	1,155[a]
2010	700
2011	649
2012	650
2013	616

Source: HUD Congressional Budget Justifications from FY2005 through FY2015. Enacted funding figures are taken from subsequent years' justifications. FY2013 funding levels reflect sequestration.

Note: Figures show total funding for the Native American Housing Block Grants account. In addition to funding the block grants, this account also includes funding for the Title VI Loan Guarantee Program, funding for training and technical assistance, and funding for a national organization representing Native American housing interests (traditionally the National American Indian Housing Council).

[a] Includes $510 million provided by the American Recovery and Reinvestment Act (P.L. 111-5).

The FHA administers a variety of mortgage insurance products, including insurance for home purchase and home improvement loans, reverse mortgages to allow the elderly to remain in their homes, and loans for the purchase, repair, or construction of apartments, hospitals, and nursing homes.

The programs are administered through two program accounts—the Mutual Mortgage Insurance/Cooperative Management Housing Insurance fund account (MMI Fund) and the General Insurance/Special Risk Insurance fund account (GI/SRI Fund). The MMI Fund provides insurance for single-family mortgages. The GI/SRI fund provides insurance for mortgages on multifamily buildings, hospitals and nursing homes, and for an assortment of special purpose loans such as manufactured housing loans and home improvement loans.

Table 9. FHA Share of Home Purchase Market, FY2002-FY2012

Fiscal Year	Number of FHA-Insured Home Purchase Mortgages (000)	FHA-Insured Mortgages as a % of All Home Purchase Mortgages
2002	765	11
2003	630	8
2004	457	7
2005	323	4
2006	295	4
2007	317	6
2008	845	24
2009	1,088	33
2010	944	32
2011	760	27
2012	738	29

Source: HUD, FHA-Insured Single Family Mortgage Market Share Reports, http://portal.hud.gov/hudportal/HUD?src=/program_offices/housing/rmra/oe/rpts/fhamktsh/fhamktqtrly.

Table 9 presents the FHA share of the home purchase mortgage market for FY2002-FY2012. The share of home purchase mortgages insured by FHA was about 11% in FY2002 and then declined to a low of 4% in FY2005 and FY2006. The FHA share of home purchase mortgages increased dramatically after FY2007, reaching a high of 33% in FY2009, as the housing market experienced turmoil and FHA insured a larger number of mortgages in an overall smaller mortgage market. FHA's share of the home purchase mortgage market has decreased somewhat since its peak, but, at 29% in FY2012, it remains high by historical standards.

Department of Veterans Affairs Loan Guarantees

The Servicemen's Readjustment Act of 1944 (P.L. 78-346) established the home loan guaranty program, which is administered by the Department of Veterans Affairs (VA). The VA loan guaranty came about as an alternative to a cash bonus for veterans returning from World War II, considered less expensive than a bonus, but still a way to provide benefits to veterans.

The loan guaranty program assists veterans by insuring mortgages made by private lenders, and is available for the purchase or construction of homes as well as to refinance existing loans. The loan guaranty has expanded over the years so that it is available to (1) all veterans who fulfill specific duration of service requirements or who were released from active duty due to service-connected disabilities, (2) members of the reserves who completed at least six years of service, and (3) spouses of veterans who died in action, died of service-connected disabilities, or who died while receiving (or while being entitled to receive) benefits for certain service-connected disabilities. Under the loan guaranty, the VA agrees to reimburse lenders for a portion of losses if borrowers default. Unlike insurance provided through the Federal Housing Administration (FHA) insurance program, the VA does not insure 100% of the loan, and instead the percentage of the loan that is guaranteed is based on the principal balance of the loan.

Table 10 presents VA-insured mortgages' share of the home purchase mortgage market for FY2002 to FY2012. The total number of VA-insured purchase loans originated per year as a share of all home purchase mortgages has increased from between 2% and 3% in FY2002-FY2007, to 8% in FY2012.

Department of Agriculture Rural Housing Loans

Through the Section 502 Rural Housing Loan program, USDA is authorized to make both direct loans and to guarantee private loans to very low- to moderate-income rural residents for the purchase or repair of new or existing single-family homes. (The program is codified at 42 U.S.C. §1472.) The direct loans have a 33-year term and interest rates may be as low as 1%. Borrowers in rural areas with incomes at or below 80% of area median income qualify for the direct loans. The guaranteed loans have 30-year terms, and borrowers in rural areas with incomes at or below 115% of the area median qualify. Priority for both direct and guaranteed loans is given to first-time homebuyers, and USDA may require that borrowers complete a homeownership counseling program.

Table 10. VA Share of Mortgage Market, FY2002-FY2012

Fiscal Year	Number of VA-Insured Home Purchase Mortgages (000)	VA-Insured Purchase Mortgages as a % of All Home Purchase Mortgages
2002	177	3
2003	149	2
2004	152	2
2005	119	2
2006	123	2
2007	118	2
2008	142	4
2009	181	5
2010	193	7
2011	187	7
2012	202	8

Source: The number of VA-insured mortgages are from VA Annual Benefits Reports. Total market data taken from HUD's website at http://www.hud.gov/offices/hsg/rmra/oe/rpts/fhamktsh/fhamkt_current.pdf. Percentages calculated by CRS.

Through the Section 504 program, the USDA makes loans and grants to very low-income homeowners (those with incomes at or below 50% of area median income) for home repairs or improvements, or to remove health and safety hazards. (The program is codified at 42 U.S.C. §1474.) The Section 504 grants may be available to homeowners who are age 62 or older. To qualify for the grants, the elderly homeowners must lack the ability to repay the full cost of the repairs. Depending on the cost of the repairs and the income of the elderly homeowner, the owner may be eligible either for a grant that will cover the full cost of the repairs, or for some combination of loan and grant.

Table 11 presents the number of mortgages that were made under the Section 502 Direct Loan Program and the Section 502 Guaranteed Loan Program in each fiscal year between FY2002 and FY2012.

Federal Home Loan Banks

The Federal Home Loan Banks (FHLB; the Banks) were created in 1932 by the Federal Home Loan Bank Act (P.L. 72-304) to serve as lenders to savings and loan associations, which at the time made the majority of home mortgage loans. The Banks were established to ensure the liquidity of these lenders, and today lend money to commercial banks, credit unions, and insurance companies in addition to savings and loans. The FHLB System includes twelve regional wholesale Banks and an Office of Finance. Each Bank is a separate legal entity, cooperatively owned by its member financial institutions, and has its own management, employees, and board of directors. Each Bank is assigned a distinct geographic area.

The FHLB system is a government-sponsored enterprise (GSE). As a GSE, the Banks receive certain privileges to assist them in carrying out their mission, such as an exemption from certain taxes.

Table 11. Number of USDA Section 502 Mortgages, FY2002-FY2012

Fiscal Year	Number of USDA Section 502 Direct Loans (000)	Number of USDA Section 502 Guaranteed Loans (000)
2002	14	28
2003	13	32
2004	15	34
2005	12	31
2006	12	30
2007	11	34
2008	10	59
2009	12	131
2010	17	133
2011	9	121
2012	8	145

Source: Housing Assistance Council data on the USDA Rural Development programs' historical activity, http://ruralhome.org/information-and-publications/rural-development-obligations/rd-data-gen/189-historicactivity.

Notes: FY2009 and FY2010 figures include loans funded under the American Recovery and Reinvestment Act (ARRA).

Each of the Federal Home Loan Banks is required to annually contribute 10% of its net income toward an Affordable Housing Program (AHP).[23] Through the AHP, the Banks provide grants and subsidized loans for rental and owner-occupied housing for very low- and low-income households. Each FHLB may set aside up to the greater of 35% of its AHP funds or $4.5 million per year to help low- and moderate-income households purchase homes by providing grants for down payment or closing cost assistance or other costs related to buying or rehabilitating a home. At least one-third of the amount set aside for homeownership assistance must be used for first-time homebuyers, and the maximum per-household grant amount may not exceed $15,000.[24]

Each of the Banks also operates a Community Investment Program (CIP). Through the CIP, the Banks offer advances to member financial institutions at discounted interest rates to fund rental and owner-occupied housing for households at or below 115% of area median income as well as other community development activities. (The Affordable Housing Program and Community Investment Program are codified at 12 U.S.C. §1430. Regulations are at 12 C.F.R. Part 1291 and 12 C.F.R. Part 952, respectively.)

Section 235

The Section 235 program, enacted as part of the Housing and Urban Development Act of 1968 (P.L. 90-448), helped to subsidize the home purchases of individual borrowers. Through the program, FHA provided a monthly subsidy payment to lenders in order to reduce the interest liability of loans made to eligible borrowers. As originally enacted and administered, homebuyers were required to pay at least 20% of their income toward debt service on their mortgages, and FHA paid the lenders the lesser of (1) the balance of the monthly payment due after the borrowers paid 20% of their income or (2) the difference between the required payments at the FHA interest rate and the payments that would be due on a loan with a 1% interest rate. As a result, the subsidy to homeowners varied depending upon their income, the amount of the mortgage, and the market interest rate.

The Section 235 program had a two-tiered eligibility component. At least 80% of program funds were made available for homebuyers with incomes that did not exceed 135% of the maximum income for admission to public housing. Applicants in this group could purchase homes with down payments as low as $200. The remaining 20% of program funds were available for a higher income group. Applicants in this group had to make down payments of at least 3% of the sales price. New commitments under the Section 235 program were halted by the 1973 Nixon moratorium; a revised version of the program was reactivated in 1976. The Section 235 program was terminated as of October 1, 1989 by the Housing and Community Development Act of 1987 (P.L. 100-242); however, according to the most recent publicly available HUD data, several thousand families continue to be assisted by the program.[25]

Mortgage Interest Deduction

Homeownership promotion has generally taken two forms: government assistance in the financing of home purchases, and tax preferences favoring homeowners. One of the tax incentives that promote homeownership is the mortgage interest deduction. The mortgage interest deduction allows homeowners to deduct any interest paid on their mortgage from their taxable income, thus reducing their tax liability. The deduction benefits those households that own homes, that have a mortgage on which they pay interest, that have federal income tax liability, and for whom itemized deductions exceed the standard deduction (approximately 75% of taxpayers take the standard deduction). It is not targeted to lower-income households.

Although the mortgage interest deduction was not initially created to promote homeownership,[26] today, the mortgage interest deduction could be considered the federal government's largest housing program. In FY2013, the Joint Committee on Taxation estimated that the mortgage interest deduction would result in a $69.7 billion tax expenditure.[27]

ISSUES AND TRENDS IN HOUSING ASSISTANCE PROGRAMS

Incidence of Housing Problems

When the federal housing assistance programs began in the 1930s, the nation was considered to be ill-housed. The Housing Act of 1937 identified an "acute shortage of decent, safe, and sanitary dwellings." Thanks in part to stricter building codes and standards, most housing in the United States today is decent, safe, and sanitary. Although some units are still considered substandard, today the greatest perceived housing problem is affordability. Housing is considered "affordable" if it costs no more than 30% of a household's income. Households that pay half or more of their income toward their housing costs are considered severely cost burdened; households that pay between 30% and 50% of their income toward their housing costs are considered moderately cost burdened. According to data from the Census Bureau's American Community Survey, 21.7 million households were moderately cost burdened and 20.6 million households were severely cost burdened in 2011.[28]

Public policy is generally most concerned with the housing affordability problems of the lowest-income families, because high housing costs may prevent these families from meeting their other basic needs. The American

Community Survey data show that in 2011, among households with income below $15,000 per year, 68.7% were severely cost burdened (compared to 62.6% in 2001), and for households with income between $15,000 and $29,999 per year, 30.9% were severely cost burdened (compared to 23.1% in 2001).[29]

HUD is directed to report to Congress periodically on the incidence of "worst case" housing needs. Worst case housing needs are defined as occurring when unassisted renters with very low incomes (at or below 50% of area median income) pay more than half of their income for housing costs or live in severely substandard housing. In its 2011 report to Congress on worst case housing needs, HUD found that nearly 8.5 million households (or 7.4% of all households) had worst case housing needs, increasing by 19% compared to 2009 (when 7.1 million households had worst case housing needs, or 6.0% of all households) and by 43% compared to 2007 (when 5.9 million households had worst case housing needs, or 5.3% of all households).[30] Prior to 2005, the percentage of households having worst case housing needs had remained relatively steady— roughly 5% of all households—since HUD began reporting on worst case housing needs in 1991. The vast majority of households with worst case housing needs in 2011 (93%) were severely cost burdened, but lived in standard housing; only about 3% of households had worst case housing needs solely because they lived in substandard housing (another 4% experienced both conditions).

Characteristics of Families Receiving Assistance

Public housing, Section 8 vouchers, and the Section 8 project-based rental assistance programs combined serve roughly 4 million households and can be considered the primary housing assistance programs for low-income families. These three forms of assistance are similar in many ways. They all target assistance to extremely low-income families, require families to pay 30% of their incomes toward rent, and generally have long waiting lists for assistance. However, the three vary in terms of their evolution, the structure of their benefit (a portable voucher versus a housing unit), and their administration (PHA versus private owner).

The similarities and differences in the programs themselves result in similarities and differences in the characteristics of the households they serve. *Table 12* provides household characteristics data for participants in the Section

8 tenant-based voucher program, the public housing program, and the project-based Section 8 rental assistance program.

The Section 8 (tenant-based) voucher program serves more single, female-headed households with children than do the public housing program or project-based programs. Based on 2012 HUD data, 44% of voucher households were households with children headed by females, compared to 34% of public housing households and 27% of project-based households. The project-based Section 8 program primarily serves families headed by persons who are elderly or live with disabilities, who account for nearly two-thirds (63%) of all households served in the program.

Table 12. Characteristics of Households Served in Selected Housing Assistance Programs

	Tenant-Based Section 8	*Public Housing*	*Project-Based Section 8*
Household Characteristics			
Elderly Head of Household or Spouse	21%	32%	46%
Non-elderly Disabled Head of Household or Spouse	28%	20%	17%
All Households with Children	49%	39%	30%
Female Head of Household	81%	74%	73%
Female Head of Household With Children	44%	34%	27%
Race and Ethnicity (Head of Household)			
Non-Hispanic White	34%	26%	45%
Non-Hispanic Black	47%	45%	34%
Hispanic	16%	25%	16%
Other	4%	3%	5%
Household Income			
$0-$5,000	14%	14%	16%
$5,001-$10,000	30%	32%	32%
$10,001-$15,000	24%	20%	26%
$15,001-$20,000	14%	13%	14%
$20,001-$30,000	12%	11%	9%
$30,001-$90,000	5%	11%	3%

Source: Calculated by CRS, based on 2012 HUD Public Use Microdata, accessed March, 2014. Totals may not add to 100% due to rounding.

This is not surprising given that owners of project-based housing may designate entire properties for elderly or disabled households. In addition, units of Section 202 housing for the elderly that were developed during the 1970s and 1980s were subsidized with project-based Section 8 rental assistance. Public housing and the Section 8 voucher program each have about half of households (52% and 49%, respectively) where the head or spouse is elderly or a person with a disability.

HUD reports race and ethnicity of the head of household as non-Hispanic white, non-Hispanic black, Hispanic, and other. In Public Housing and the Section 8 voucher program, non-Hispanic black household heads make up the largest share of households (45% and 47%, respectively). In the project-based Section 8 program, non-Hispanic white household heads are the largest share (45%), with non-Hispanic black household heads making up 34% of the total. Between 16% and 25% of households served across the three programs have heads of household who identify their ethnicity as Hispanic, with Public Housing having the largest share.

The rules governing the three main housing assistance programs require that they serve low-income households, those with incomes at or below 80% of area median income. However, with the targeting required in these programs, many households served have very low- or extremely low-incomes (at or below 50% or 30% of area median income, respectively).[31] As an example, in 2012 the national median income was $65,000,[32] meaning that low-income would be considered at or below $49,200; very low-income, $32,500; and extremely low-income, $19,500. The majority of households served in each of the three programs have incomes at or below $15,000. In Public Housing, the percentage of households with incomes at or below $15,000 is 65%, rising to 68% of households in the Section 8 voucher program, and 73% of households in Project-Based Section 8.

Concern has been raised that perhaps the income-based rent structure in the assisted housing programs acts as a disincentive for households to increase their earnings; for every new dollar a family earns, thirty-cents must go toward rent.[33] There have been some efforts to mitigate this perceived work disincentive, including the adoption of an earned income disregard in the public housing program and an earned income disregard for disabled families in the voucher program. Congress also developed the Family Self Sufficiency (FSS) program in an effort to promote work. Families in the FSS program enter into contracts with their PHAs in which they agree to take steps toward becoming self-sufficient within five years. The PHA, in turn, agrees to deposit any increased rent collected as a result of the family's increased earnings into an escrow account that the family will receive at the end of the five years, or from which they can make interim withdrawals for approved purposes. FSS is voluntary for PHAs to administer and voluntary for families to join.

The Federal Government's Role in Affordable Rental Housing

Beginning in the 1980s, the federal government took on a lesser role in the creation of assisted housing. This occurred in several ways. Congress ceased funding new construction under the Section 8 project-based program, which from its enactment in 1974 had subsidized hundreds of thousands of units of assisted housing. This left very few active programs in which HUD supported the development of physical housing units. Between 1976 and 1982, the federal housing programs produced more than 1 million units of subsidized housing.[34] In the following years, however, annual production was around 25,000 new subsidized units.[35] Around the time that housing production was declining, Congress created two programs that gave a good deal of control over decisions regarding housing policy and development to state and local governments—these included the Low Income Housing Tax Credit (LIHTC) program and the HOME Investment Partnerships program. These programs, particularly the LIHTC, have been used by states and localities to create hundreds of thousands of units of affordable housing.

The federal government's decision to take a lesser role in the development of housing has had several consequences. First, state and local governments have taken on an increased role in providing affordable housing and establishing priorities in their communities.[36] Second, due to a reduction in the number of new affordable housing units that are created each year, the need to preserve existing affordable housing units has taken on a new importance. A third consequence is the need for multiple streams of funding other than federal grants in order both to support the creation of new affordable housing units and to preserve existing units. Those three consequences are discussed more fully below.

First, with the advent of both the LIHTC program and the HOME program, states and localities were able to exercise discretion in determining how to prioritize and develop housing using a larger pool of federal funds. Until that point, even though states, through their Housing Finance Agencies, helped finance mortgage loans and affordable rental housing, their role was limited by the amount of funds available.

In the Low Income Housing Tax Credit program, states develop plans in which they may set aside a certain percentage of tax credits for populations such as homeless individuals or persons with disabilities. They may also decide to use tax credits to preserve existing housing as well as to build new housing. Funds that states receive from the HOME program may be used for the construction of new rental housing and rental assistance for low-income households. A potential drawback of these programs is their inability, on their own, to reach the neediest households.[37] For example, in a LIHTC development, at least 20% of units must be affordable to households at or below 50% of area median income, or 40% of units must be affordable to households at or below 60% of area median income. Many of the older HUD programs constructed housing that was affordable to households at or below 30% of area median income—those considered extremely low-income. Often these households cannot afford units in LIHTC properties without rental subsidies, such as Section 8 vouchers.[38]

Another way some states and local governments support affordable housing is outside of the assistance of the federal government, through establishment of their own housing trust funds. These trust funds use dedicated funding sources such as document recording fees or real estate transfer taxes to create a pool of funds for affordable housing. By using a dedicated source of financing, trust funds may not be as subject to the vicissitudes of state budgets as are other means of funding housing development. States and local communities also support affordable housing through inclusionary zoning. Through this method, housing developers are expected to dedicate a percentage of units they build as affordable housing. In exchange, states or local communities give developers incentives that allow them to expand or speed up the pace of development. Some of the incentives include density bonuses or zoning variances that allow developers to build larger facilities than they would be able to under existing zoning regulations, as well as expedited approval of building permits.

A second consequence of the decreased role of the federal government in the production of affordable housing units is the increased pressure to maintain the affordability of existing units. Many HUD subsidized units that were developed in the 1960s and 1970s through programs such as Section 236 and Section 221(d)(3), as well as those units that received Section 8 project-based rental assistance, are no longer available to low-income households. At the time the properties were developed, building owners entered into contracts with HUD in which they agreed to maintain affordability for a certain number of years. The duration of these contracts varied; depending on the federal program, these contracts, or "use restrictions" may last between 15 years (the Low Income Housing Tax Credit program) and 50 years (early Section 202 developments). In recent years, these contracts have begun to expire or, in some cases, property owners have chosen to pay off their mortgages early and end the use restrictions. Contracts for rental assistance, including project-based Section 8 rental assistance, have also begun to expire. When any of these events occur, owners may charge market-rate rents for the units, and the affordable units are lost. The term used to refer to efforts to maintain the affordability of these housing units is "affordable housing preservation." In coming years, more and more property owners will be in a position to opt out of affordability restrictions and thousands of units could be lost.[39]

Congress has attempted to enact laws that would preserve affordable housing units; however, due to the temporary nature of some of the measures, preservation remains a concern. Congress first enacted legislation to help preserve affordable rental housing in 1987. The Emergency Low-Income Housing Preservation Act (ELIHPA), enacted as part of the Housing and Community Development Act of 1987 (P.L. 100-242), was a temporary measure that prevented owners of Section 236 and Section 221(d)(3) properties from prepaying their mortgages. In 1990, the Low-Income Housing Preservation and Resident Homeownership Act (LIHPRHA), enacted as part of the Cranston-Gonzalez National Affordable Housing Act (P.L. 101-625), offered incentives to owners to keep them from prepaying their mortgages. However, six years after LIHPRHA was enacted, Congress reinstated the right of owners to prepay their mortgages. (See P.L. 104-134.) Another effort to preserve affordable housing was enacted as part of the Multifamily Assisted Housing Reform and Accountability Act (MAHRA, P.L. 105-65). Through this effort, HUD restructures the debt of building owners while at the same time renegotiating their rental assistance contracts. Unlike ELIHPA and LIHPRHA, MAHRA is still in effect.

A third consequence of the decreased federal role in the production of affordable housing is the need for low-income housing developers to bring together multiple funding streams in order to build a development. When the federal government first began to subsidize the production of affordable housing, in many cases the funds appropriated for housing programs were sufficient to construct or rehabilitate the affordable units without the need for funds from the private financial markets. Over the years, however, federal programs that provide grants for the construction of multifamily housing for low-income households have become a smaller portion of the government's housing portfolio. At the same time, the grants themselves have become a smaller portion of the total amount needed to support the development of affordable housing. As a result, it has become necessary for developers to turn to multiple sources of financing, including Low Income Housing Tax Credits, tax exempt bonds, and state or local housing trust funds. In addition, it is often necessary for building owners to seek rent subsidies through programs like Section 8 and HOME to make renting to very low- or extremely low-income households feasible.

The interactions among these various financing streams can be complex, and putting together a development plan may require the expertise of housing finance professionals.

Shift to Tenant-Based Assistance

Over time, the number of Section 8 vouchers provided and funded by the federal government has grown, while the number of federally-subsidized housing units—through project-based Section 8 rental assistance and public housing—has declined.[40] This change from project-based assistance to tenant-based assistance is due, in part, to Congress' decision to increase the voucher program by creating new vouchers after new construction in the project-based Section 8 program and public housing program had been halted.[41] Some of these vouchers were general purpose vouchers, available to any eligible family, and some were special purpose vouchers, targeted to special populations, such as families transitioning from welfare to work and homeless veterans.

This shift is also due, in part, to declines in the number of project-based assistance and public housing units. As previously noted in this report, the project-based rental assistance contracts between private landlords and HUD began expiring in the 1980s. When these contracts expire, private property owners can either renew their contracts with HUD (typically on an annual or five-year basis) or leave the program. When property owners leave the program, their tenants typically receive Section 8 vouchers—referred to as tenant protection vouchers. As also noted earlier in this report, since the mid-1990s, when public housing units are demolished or sold, PHAs are not required to replace each lost unit with a new public housing unit. Instead, displaced families who are not relocated to other public housing units are provided with tenant-protection vouchers.

Also contributing to the decline in Public Housing units is the Rental Assistance Demonstration (RAD) program, enacted as part of the FY2012

Consolidated Appropriations Act (P.L. 112-55). Through RAD, PHAs may convert funds received through the Public Housing operating and capital funds to either project-based Section 8 rental assistance or project-based vouchers. As of the date of this report, the number of eligible Public Housing units eligible to convert through RAD was capped at 60,000.

The shift from project-based assistance to tenant-based assistance has several implications for families. Vouchers offer portability, which, for some residents of public or other assisted housing, may mean the ability to move out of a troubled community to a community with new opportunities. However, there is debate over whether vouchers' portability leads to economic or social mobility. Early research on mobility showed promise that families—particularly, low-income black families—that moved from heavily poverty- and minority-concentrated public housing neighborhoods to more economically- and racially-integrated neighborhoods using vouchers could see improved employment and child outcomes.[42] However, more recent mobility research has shown mixed results.[43] There is also some evidence that, for families accustomed to living in public housing, the transition to the private market rental market with a voucher can be difficult without counseling and other supports, which may not be consistently provided.[44]

Supporting Homeownership

For 2013, the Census Bureau reported a U.S. homeownership rate of 65.1%, down from a peak of 69% in 2004.[45] However, the distribution of homeownership is not even. The rate is highest in the Midwest (69.7%) and lowest in the West (59.4%). It is highest for those age 65 years or more (80.8%), and lowest for those under 35 years old (36.8%). It is higher for whites (73.3%) than it is for blacks (43.1%). Hispanics, who can be of any race, had a homeownership rate of 46.1%. The homeownership rate is higher for those with income at or greater than the median (about 80%) and lower for those with incomes less than the median (about 50%).[46]

The federal government has historically provided support for homeownership through a variety of programs and activities. These include favorable treatment in the tax code (mortgage interest and property tax deductions); the creation and favorable treatment of certain lending institutions that make home loans (Federal Home Loan Banks); the establishment of federal programs that insure lenders against losses on home loans (through FHA, VA, and USDA); establishing institutions that create a secondary market for mortgages and enable funds for mortgages to be available throughout the U.S. (Fannie Mae, Freddie Mac, and Ginnie Mae); establishing counseling programs, within HUD and other agencies, that fund organizations that counsel prospective homebuyers on obtaining and maintaining homeownership; and funding grant programs that provide down payment and closing cost assistance to some homebuyers.

While not all of these initiatives were established specifically to promote homeownership, many policy makers have come to view these programs and activities as important for helping households access affordable financing to purchase a home. Homeownership has long been perceived to provide a number of economic and social benefits, including an opportunity to build wealth through accumulating home equity and a greater level of neighborhood satisfaction and community involvement.[47] Given these perceived benefits, an ongoing policy concern has been that some creditworthy households might be unable to achieve these benefits due to difficulties obtaining affordable mortgages. For example, it may be difficult for some households who have the income to sustain a mortgage but do not have funds to make a large down payment to access mortgages on affordable terms.

Since the 1940s, nearly every U.S. President has expressed support for the concept of increased homeownership. For example, there has been the George H.W. Bush Administration's "Blueprint for the American Dream," the Clinton Administration's "National Homeownership Strategy," and the George W. Bush Administration's "Homeownership Initiative." Generally, these proposals involved little new federal funding, but sought to rally the private sector to use existing programs to reach some specified target. The primary focus of the more recent proposals was to increase homeownership among groups who have traditionally been less likely to be homeowners, such as low-income families and minorities.

Given the unprecedented downturn in U.S. housing and mortgage markets in recent years, and the resultant high foreclosure rate, the future of federal policy promoting homeownership is uncertain. High foreclosure rates and steep house price decreases in some areas have led some to question the traditional rationales for promoting homeownership. Nonetheless, others continue to believe that federal policy should continue to support activities that could increase access to homeownership for creditworthy borrowers. Given this policy debate, it remains to be seen whether, and to what extent, the federal government will pursue policies to encourage higher rates of homeownership in the future.

DATA

The following tables present data on federal spending (outlays) on selected housing assistance programs as well as data on the number of assisted units, since 1980.

Table 13 presents outlays for selected programs, in both real and nominal dollars. It is important to note that this table does not include any spending information related to loan commitments or obligations. As can be seen in *Table 13*, outlays for the selected programs have increased, in both real and nominal dollars, over the more than three decades presented (a 377% increase in nominal dollars, a 95% increase in real dollars).

Table 13. Outlays, Selected Housing Programs, FY1980-FY2013 (dollars in millions)

Fiscal Year	PublicAss-istance[a]	Rental Housing[b]	Other Housing Assistance[c]	Block Grants[d,e]	Homeless and HOPWA[f]	Total Nominal Dollars	Total 2013 Dollars
1980	2,104	2,185	1,042	3,910	—[g]	9,240	22,564
1981	3,115	2,401	1,139	4,048	—[g]	10,703	23,809
1982	4,085	2,574	1,208	3,795	—[g]	11,661	24,273
1983	4,995	3,206	1,107	3,557	—[g]	12,865	25,648
1984	6,030	2,821	1,037	3,823	—[g]	13,711	26,404
1985	6,818	3,408	952	3,820	—[g]	14,998	27,954
1986	7,430	2,882	890	3,329	—[g]	14,530	26,478
1987	8,125	2,161	868	2,970	2	14,125	25,178
1988	9,133	2,526	851	3,054	37	15,601	26,941
1989	9,918	3,043	774	2,951	70	16,756	27,828
1990	10,581	3,918	778	2,821	82	18,180	29,136
1991	11,400	4,544	712	2,981	120	19,757	30,578
1992	12,307	5,045	752	3,099	145	21,347	32,250
1993	13,289	6,296	752	3,416	172	23,924	35,304
1994	14,576	6,771	762	4,439	189	26,737	38,614
1995	16,948	7,414	750	5,519	270	30,901	43,700
1996	15,779	7,605	719	5,761	453	30,317	42,090
1997	16,393	7,687	738	5,731	718	31,267	42,656
1998[h]	16,114	7,534	717	6,360	916	31,640	42,639
1999	15,652	6,560	693	6,748	1,032	30,685	40,834
2000	16,692	7,193	667	7,077	1,100	32,729	42,672
2001	17,494	7,483	659	7,047	1,208	33,892	43,145
2002	19,394	8,193	644	7,349	1,358	36,937	46,279

Table 13. (Continued)

Fiscal Year	PublicAss-istance[a]	Rental Housing[b]	Other Housing Assistance[c]	Block Grants[d,e]	Homeless and HOPWA[f]	Total Nominal Dollars	Total 2013 Dollars
2003	21,941	7,837	630	7,229	1,376	39,013	47,962
2004	23,453	7,490	620	7,113	1,492	40,168	48,189
2005	24,495	7,426	603	7,225	1,562	41,312	48,052
2006	24,756	7,225	569	7,086	1,655	41,292	46,516
2007	25,674	7,295	559	7,011	1,664	42,202	46,290
2008	25,796	7,534	579	6,828	1,754	42,491	45,664
2009	26,351	7,973	556	6,565	1,801	43,246	45,936
2010	28,848	9,997	519	8,041	2,320	49,725	52,362
2011	29,677	8,973	494	8,463	2,616	50,223	51,874
2012	29,119	7,068	445	7,407	2,288	46,326	47,026
2013	29,004	6,367	391	6,307	2,042	44,111	44,111

Source: Table prepared by CRS based on data from the Department of Housing and Urban Development Annotated Tables for the 2001 Budget, Congressional Budget Justifications, and the Office of Management and Budget's Public Budget Database. Real dollars are obtained using the GDP deflator in the President's FY2015 budget, Table 10.1. The table includes outlays of funds provided as part of the American Recovery and Reinvestment Act.

[a] Rental Assistance includes project- and tenant-based Section 8, Section 202, and Section 811.

[b] Public Housing includes Public Housing Capital Fund, Public Housing Operating Fund, Public Housing Drug Elimination Program, and HOPE VI.

[c] Other Housing Assistance includes Section 235, Section 236, and Rent Supplement.

[d] Block Grants includes funding for the Community Development Fund, including the Community Development Block Grant (CDBG), HOME Investment Partnerships Program, Native American Housing Block Grants and Housing Counseling Assistance.

[e] Congress periodically provides emergency funding through the CDBG program following disasters, generally in amounts less than $1 billion per year. However, on some occasions in recent years, Congress provided substantially more funding. Following the September 11, 2001 terrorist attacks Congress appropriated $3 billion for CDBG, following the 2005 hurricanes, more than $16 billion, and in the aftermath of Hurricane Sandy, in 2012, $15 billion. As a result, total block grant outlays from FY2002 through FY2013 do not include CDBG emergency funding.

[f] Homeless includes HOPWA and the Homeless Assistance Grants.

[g] Neither the Homeless Assistance Grants nor the HOPWA program existed prior to FY1987.

[h] Prior to FY1998, funding for the Native American housing programs that were consolidated by NAHASDA was included in other accounts.

Table 14 presents the number of units eligible for payment across several programs through FY2009. Unit data are not provided from FY2010 to the present because HUD no longer reports the number of units eligible for payment and could not provide the information to CRS. HUD, as part of its Annual Performance Reports, publishes data on households in occupied rental housing units receiving assistance. However, the data are not comparable to those provided in *Table 14.*

Units eligible for payment is a measure of the number of housing units under rental assistance contracts with HUD (project-based Section 8, Section 202 and Section 811 units, and rental assistance payment and rent supplement units) as well as the number of Section 8 vouchers. Generally, over the course of a year, each unit will be available for one household, although given turnover, properties are rarely at 100% occupancy and vouchers are rarely 100% utilized. As a result, fewer households receive assistance in a year than there are units eligible for payment in a year.

As shown in *Table 14*, the total number of units eligible for payment under the selected housing programs has grown by over 50% over the nearly three decades presented. However, most of that growth happened in the 1980s. Since the early 1990s, the number of units eligible for payment has gone up and down from year to year, with an overall decline in units from FY2001 to FY2009.

Table 14 also helps to illustrate the trend away from public housing and other housing assistance to rental assistance (Section 8 vouchers) discussed earlier in this report. The number of units assisted under the other housing assistance programs has been on the decline since the Nixon Moratorium in the 1970s. For many of those units, once the family leaves the program, they receive a voucher. In the case of public housing, the number of units continued to increase until the mid-1990s, as contracted units became available. Since the mid-1990s, through the HOPE VI program and other authority, PHAs have been demolishing and disposing of many of their public housing developments. In their place, some replacement public housing units have been built, but many of the units were replaced with Section 8 vouchers.

Table 14. Units Eligible for Payment, Selected Housing Programs, FY1980-FY2009

Fiscal Year	Rental Assistance[a]	Public Housing	Other Housing Assistance[b,c]	Annual Total
1980	1,153,311	1,192,000	761,759	3,107,070
1981	1,318,927	1,204,000	774,524	3,297,451
1982	1,526,683	1,224,000	757,213	3,507,896
1983	1,749,904	1,250,000	663,424	3,663,328
1984	1,909,812	1,331,908	617,956	3,859,676
1985	2,010,306	1,355,152	577,780	3,943,238
1986	2,143,339	1,379,679	553,765	4,076,783
1987[d]	2,239,503	1390,098	521,651	4,151,252
1988[d]	2,332,462	1,397,907	496,961	4,227,330
1989[d]	2,419,866	1,403,816	491,635	4,315,317
1990	2,500,462	1,404,870	481,033	4,386,365
1991	2,547,995	1,410,137	473,945	4,432,077
1992	2,796,613	1,409,191	428,986	4,634,790
1993	2,812,008	1,407,923	434,498	4,654,429
1994	2,925,959	1,409,455	413,999	4,749,413
1995	2,911,692	1,397,205	415,165	4,724,062
1996	2,958,162	1,388,746	404,498	4,751,406
1997	2,943,634	1,372,260	385,651	4,701,545
1998[e]	3,000,935	1,295,437	359,884	4,656,256
1999[f]	2,985,339	1,273,500	337856	4,596,695
2000	3,196,225	1,266,980	302,898	4,766,103
2001	3,396,289	1,219,238	262,343	4,877,870
2002	3,420,669	1,208,730	233,736	4,863,135
2003	3,476,451	1,206,721	179,952	4,863,124
2004	3,508,091	1,188,649	155,289	4,852,029
2005	3,483,511	1,162,808	128,771	4,775,090
2006[g]	3,498,363	1,172,204	123,503	4,794,070
2007	3,532,079	1,155,377	100,595	4,788,051
2008	3,495,299	1,140,294	109,773	4,745,366
2009	3,528,620	1,128,891	97,862	4,755,373

Source: Table prepared by CRS based on data from the Department of Housing and Urban Development Annotated Tables for the 2001 Budget and Congressional Budget Justifications, Housing Payments.

Note: Unit data are not provided from FY2010 to the present because HUD no longer reports units eligible for payment and could not provide this data to CRS. HUD, as part of its Annual Performance Reports, publishes data on households in occupied rental housing units receiving assistance. However, the data are not comparable to those provided.

[a] Rental Assistance includes Section 8, Section 202, Section 811.

[b] Other Housing Assistance includes Section 235, Section 236, Rent Supplement.

[c] Total is adjusted for units receiving multiple subsidies.

[d] Voucher counts for FY1987-FY1989 reflect vouchers leased, rather than reserved (contracted) vouchers.

[e] Prior to FY1998, Native American public housing units were included in the count of public housing units. Beginning in 1998, those units are not included in the public housing unit count.

[f] The voucher count in FY1999 reflects obligated vouchers, rather than reserved (contracted) vouchers.

[g] Beginning in FY2006, HUD reported the total number of "funded" vouchers, which is HUD's estimate of how many vouchers the amount of funding provided by Congress would sustain, given the distribution of that funding.

End Notes

[1] For more information on the history of public housing, see Robert Moore Fisher, 20 Years of Public Housing (Harper and Brothers, 1959) and Wood, Elizabeth, The Beautiful Beginnings, the Failure to Learn: Fifty Years of Public Housing in America, The National Center for Housing Management, October 1982.

[2] Peter Dreir, "Labor's Love Lost? Rebuilding Unions' Involvement in Federal Housing Policy," Housing Policy Debate, vol. 2, no. 2, p. 327.

[3] President Harry S. Truman, State of the Union Address, January 5, 1949.

[4] See, for example, Committee on Banking and Currency, report to accompany S. 1922, the Housing Act of 1961, 87th Cong., 1st sess., S.Rept. 281, May 19, 1961 ("The largest unfilled demand in the housing market is that of moderate-income families.").

[5] S.Rept. 281. "Perhaps the most significant reason that previous proposals to establish a moderate-income housing program have not been favorably received by the Congress is that the majority of those proposals would have placed sole responsibility for such a program on the Federal Government."

[6] U.S. Department of Housing and Urban Development, Multifamily Properties: Opting In, Opting Out and Remaining Affordable, January 2006, p. 1, available at http://www.huduser.org/Publications/pdf/opting_in.pdf.

[7] U.S. Department of Housing and Urban Development, Housing for the Elderly and Handicapped: The Experience of the Section 202 Program from 1959 to 1977, January 1979, p. 17.

[8] U.S. Congress, Senate Committee on Banking, Housing and Urban Affairs, Subcommittee on Housing and Urban Affairs, An Analysis of the Section 235 and 236 Programs, committee print, 93rd Cong., 1st sess., May 24, 1973, p. 9, available at http://www.congress.gov/crsx/products-nd/73.1142.doc.pdf.

[9] U.S. Department of Housing and Urban Development, "FY1974 Budget Summary, Housing Production and Mortgage Credit," p. 7.

[10] HUD, "Annotated Tables for 2001 Budget," p. 86.

[11] President Richard Nixon, Presidential Message to Congress on Housing Policy, September 19, 1973.

[12] The National Housing Task Force, A Decent Place to Live, March 1988, available from S.Hrg. 100-689. See p. 142.

[13] See A Decent Place to Live, available at S.Hrg. 100-689, p. 142.

[14] Ibid., pp. 154-155. See also Michael A. Stegman and J. David Holden, Non-federal Housing Programs: How States and Localities Are Responding to Federal Cutbacks in Low-Income Housing (Washington, DC: The Urban Land Institute, 1987).

[15] Ibid. See also Charles J. Orlebeke, "The Evolution of Low-Income Housing Policy, 1949 to 1999," Housing Policy Debate, vol. 11, no. 2 (2000), pp. 509-510, available at http://www.mi.vt.edu/data/files/hpd%2011(2)/ hpd%2011(2)_orlebeke.pdf.

[16] Karl E. Case, "Investors, Developers, and Supply-Side Subsidies: How Much is Enough?" Housing Policy Debate, vol. 2, no. 2 (April 1990), pp. 349-351, available at http://www.mi.vt.edu/data/files/hpd%202(2)/ hpd%202(2)%20case.pdf.

[17] For more information, see the final report of the National Commission on Severely Distressed Public Housing, 1992.

[18] "Handicapped" families were added to the definition of "elderly" families in P.L. 88-560, the Housing Act of 1964. In 1990, the Cranston-Gonzalez National Affordable Housing Act (P.L. 101-625) separated housing for persons with disabilities from housing for elderly persons with the creation of the Section 811 Supportive Housing for Persons with Disabilities program.

[19] A disability is defined as (1) having a physical, mental, or emotional impairment that is expected to be of long-continued or indefinite duration, substantially impedes the ability to live independently, and could be improved by suitable housing, (2) a developmental disability. 42 U.S.C. §8013(k)(2).

[20] U.S. Department of Housing and Urban Development, Low Income Tax Credit Database, accessed March 19, 2014, http://www.huduser.org/portal/datasets/lihtc.html.

[21] Joint Committee on Taxation, Estimates of Federal Tax Expenditures for Fiscal Years 2012-2017, committee print, February 1, 2013, p. 33, https://www.jct.gov/publications.html?func=startdown&id=4503 (hereinafter Estimates of Federal Tax Expenditures for Fiscal Years 2012-2017). The Joint Committee on Taxation (JCT) measures a tax expenditure as the difference between tax liability under present law and tax liability computed without the tax expenditure provision. The JCT assumes all other tax expenditures remain in the tax code and that taxpayer behavior is unchanged. The tax expenditure estimate for the LIHTC includes tax credits taken by individuals and corporations.

[22] Ibid., p. 34.

[23] See http://www.fhlbanks.com/programs_affordhousing.htm.

[24] For more information, see the Federal Housing Finance Agency's website at http://fhfa.gov/Default.aspx?Page=102. The Federal Housing Finance Agency is the regulator for the FHLBs.

[25] HUD, Congressional Justifications for FY2011, p. K-3.

[26] As described in CRS Report R41596, The Mortgage Interest and Property Tax Deductions: Analysis and Options, by Mark P. Keightley, when the federal income tax was instituted in 1913, all interest payments were deductible, including business and personal expenses. Over

time, the ability to deduct other personal interest payments has been eliminated while the deductibility of mortgage interest was maintained.

[27] Estimates of Federal Tax Expenditures for Fiscal Years 2012-2017, p. 33. See footnote 21 for full citation.

[28] Joint Center for Housing Studies of Harvard University, The State of the Nation's Housing 2013, p. 27, http://www.jchs.harvard.edu/sites/jchs.harvard.edu/files/son2013.pdf.

[29] Ibid., Table A-3.

[30] U.S. Department of Housing and Urban Development, Worst Case Housing Needs 2011 Report to Congress, August 2013, pp. 1-2, 25, http://www.huduser.org/Publications/pdf/HUD-506_WorstCase2011_reportv3.pdf.

[31] For more information about income eligibility, see CRS Report R42734, Income Eligibility and Rent in HUD Rental Assistance Programs: Responses to Frequently Asked Questions, by Libby Perl and Maggie McCarty.

[32] U.S. Department of Housing and Urban Development, Notice PDR-12-01, Estimated Median Family Incomes for Fiscal Year 2012, December 1, 2011, http://www.huduser.org/portal/datasets/il/il12/Medians2012.pdf.

[33] Edgar Olsen et al., "Effects of Different Types of Housing Assistance on Earnings and Employment," Cityscape: A Journal of Policy Development and Research, vol. 8, no. 2, p. 2005.

[34] The National Housing Task Force, A Decent Place to Live, March 1988. See S.Hrg. 100-689, p. 142.

[35] Ibid.

[36] Michael A. Stegman, State and Local Affordable Housing Programs: A Rich Tapestry (Washington, DC: Urban Land Institute, 1999).

[37] See, for example, Recapitalization Advisors, Inc., The Low Income Housing Tax Credit Effectiveness and Efficiency: A Presentation of the Issues, March 4, 2002, p. 11, available at http://www.affordablehousinginstitute.org/resources/ library/MHC_LIHT.pdf.

[38] Ethan Handelman, Jeffrey Oakman, and David A. Smith, The Interaction of LIHTC and Section 8 Rents, Recapitalization Advisors, Inc., January 30, 2007, p. 4, available at http://www.recapadvisors.com/pdf/Wu%2061.pdf.

[39] For more information, see CRS Report R41182, Preservation of HUD-Assisted Housing, by Maggie McCarty and Libby Perl.

[40] For data on vouchers from FY1998 through FY2009, when numbers grew from 1.6 million to 2.18 million, see the Government Accountability Office Report, GAO-06-405, Rental Housing Assistance: Policy Decisions and Market Factors Explain Changes in the Costs of the Section 8 Programs, April 28, 2006 and the FY2011 HUD Congressional Budget Justifications. Note that the methodology for counting Section 8 vouchers has changed over time; therefore, the 2009 count may underestimate the number of vouchers. For data on Public Housing units, which declined from just under 1.3 million units in FY1998 to just under 1.13 million units in FY2009, see HUD Congressional Budget Justifications. And for data on project-based Section 8 rental assistance, which declined from just under 1.4 million units in CY1998 to just under 1.28 million units in FY2009, see Econometrica, et al., Multifamily Properties: Opting In, Opting Out and Remaining Affordable, January 2006 (CY1998 data, Table 2.2) and HUD Congressional Budget Justifications (FY2009 data). Note that for project-based figures, a calendar year figure is compared to a fiscal year figure.

[41] The authority to enter into new project-based Section 8 contracts was repealed in 1983 and the 1998 public housing reform law prohibited PHAs from increasing the number of public housing units under contract.

[42] J.E. Rosenbaum, Changing the Geography of Opportunity by Expanding Residential Choice: Lessons from the Gautreaux, Housing Policy Debate, vol. 6 no. 1, Fannie Mae Foundation, 1995.

[43] For more information, see CRS Report R42832, Choice and Mobility in the Housing Choice Voucher Program: Review of Research Findings and Considerations for Policymakers, by Maggie McCarty and Carmen Brick.

[44] Popkin, Susan, et al., A Decade of HOPE VI: Research Findings and Policy Challenges, Urban Institute, May 18, 2004.

[45] U.S. Department of Commerce, U.S. Census Bureau, Housing Vacancies and Homeownership Annual Statistics: 2013, Tables 14, 17, and 22. Homeownership rates by household income are from U.S. Census Bureau News, "Residential Vacancies and Homeownership in the Fourth Quarter 2013," January 31, 2014, pp. 5-10, http://www.census.gov/housing/hvs/files/qtr413/q413press.pdf.

[46] U.S. Census Bureau News, "Residential Vacancies and Homeownership in the Fourth Quarter 2013," January 31, 2014, pp. 5-10, http://www.census.gov/housing/hvs/ files/qtr413 /q413press.pdf.

[47] For example, see the discussion of possible benefits related to homeownership in Christopher E. Herbert and Eric S. Belsky, The Homeownership Experience of Low-Income and Minority Families: A Review and Synthesis of the Literature, Abt Associates, Inc., prepared for U.S. Department of Housing and Urban Development, Office of Policy Development and Research, February 2006, pp. 3-6, http://www.huduser.org/publications/ pdf/hisp _homeown9.pdf.

In: Federal Housing Assistance Programs ...
Editor: Eric Collier
ISBN: 978-1-63484-336-2

Chapter 3

AFFORDABLE RENTAL HOUSING: ASSISTANCE IS PROVIDED BY FEDERAL, STATE, AND LOCAL PROGRAMS, BUT THERE IS INCOMPLETE INFORMATION ON COLLECTIVE PERFORMANCE*

United States Government Accountability Office

WHY GAO DID THIS STUDY

The federal government, states, and localities play a significant role in providing rental assistance and developing affordable rental housing for low-income households.

This report (1) identifies the federal, state, and local government funded programs that provide rental assistance to low-income households and identifies indications of program fragmentation and overlap; (2) assesses the extent of intergovernmental collaboration for rental assistance; and (3) determines what is known about performance at the federal level, at selected state and local jurisdictions and for the collective performance of the levels of government providing rental assistance.

* This is an edited, reformatted and augmented version of a United States Government Accountability Office publication, No. GAO-15-645, dated September 2015.

GAO partnered with 25 state and local audit offices to design an audit plan that 6 participating audit offices conducted on rental assistance to low-income households. GAO assessed the completed results, reviewed documentation, and interviewed officials from HUD, Treasury, and IRS.

What GAO Recommends

GAO recommends that HUD, in consultation with the RPWG, work with states and localities to develop an approach for compiling and reporting on the collective performance of federal, state, and local rental assistance programs. HUD disagreed with the recommendation as originally drafted because it did not believe that it was addressed to the appropriate party. GAO agreed and modified the recommendation to direct it to HUD, in consultation with the RPWG. Treasury and IRS did not comment on the recommendation.

What GAO Found

The federal government and state and local entities provide both rental assistance and affordable housing through a wide variety of programs. The six participating audit offices that conducted coordinated audits on rental assistance reported that the programs they reviewed were funded solely through one level of government or were funded by a combination of resources. In February 2012, GAO found instances of fragmentation and overlap among federal rental assistance programs. In this review, GAO and the participating audit offices found indications of fragmentation and overlap among programs reported in Oregon and Washington.

The Rental Policy Working Group (RPWG), which was established in 2010 by the White House Domestic Policy Council to better coordinate federal rental policy, collaborates with state and local governments in multiple areas. The participating audit offices found that their government collaborated with other jurisdictions.

The Department of Housing and Urban Development (HUD), the Internal Revenue Service (IRS) and the participating audit offices reported on the performance of rental assistance programs to varying extents. HUD reported on its performance for only one of its two rental assistance strategic objectives, but IRS had not set goals or assessed the performance of the Low Income

Housing Tax Credit. The participating audit offices reported that most jurisdictions had performance information at both the jurisdictional and program levels. However, without information on the government-wide performance of rental assistance, the Congress, decision makers, and stakeholders at all levels of government are hampered in their ability to set priorities and allocate resources. While complete and reliable information is a vital component of assessing effectiveness, GAO recognizes it is difficult to identify relevant federal, state, and local programs; collect performance information from multiple levels of government; and synthesize the information to reflect collective performance. HUD, the nation's leading housing agency, in consultation with the RPWG, is well positioned to capitalize on its existing collaboration among federal agencies and with state and local jurisdictions.

ABBREVIATIONS

CDBG	Community Development Block Grant
DPC	Domestic Policy Council
ESG	Emergency Solutions Grant
FHA	Federal Housing Administration
GPRAMA	Government Performance and Results Act Modernization Act of 2010
HOME	HOME Investment Partnerships Program
HUD	U.S. Department of Housing and Urban Development
HFA	Housing Finance Agencies
HTF	Housing Trust Fund
INTOSAI	International Organization of Supreme Audit Institutions
IRS	Internal Revenue Service
LIHTC	Low Income Housing Tax Credit
MOU	Memoranda of Understanding
NAHMA	National Affordable Housing Management Association
NCHMA	National Council of Housing Market Analysts
NCSHA	National Council of State Housing Agencies
OMB	Office of Management and Budget
PHA	Public Housing Agencies
RPWG	Rental Policy Working Group
RD	Rural Development
RHS	Rural Housing Service

SLR	Subsidy Layering Review
Treasury	U.S. Department of the Treasury
USDA	United States Department of Agriculture

* * *

September 15, 2015

The Honorable Ron Johnson
Chairman
Committee on Homeland Security and Governmental Affairs
United States Senate

Dear Mr. Chairman,

In 2013, nearly half of the nation's 41 million renters were paying more than 30 percent of their monthly income for rent, signifying a moderate rent burden under the federal standards for affordable housing.[1] Furthermore, the nation's leading housing agency, the U.S. Department of Housing and Urban Development (HUD), reported in April that more than 7.7 million very low-income families have "worst case housing needs" because they do not receive government housing assistance and paid more than half of their monthly income for rent, lived in severely substandard housing, or both. The federal government, states, and localities play a significant role in providing rental assistance and developing affordable rental housing for low-income households.

The federal government largely subsidizes rental payments for low-income households and awards grants and tax credits to state and local governments for developing affordable housing that includes rental housing. In fiscal year 2014, HUD provided more than $36 billion in rental assistance to low-income households and in affordable housing development funding to state and local governments. 2 Funding for HUD's largest rental assistance program—Housing Choice Vouchers—mostly increased prior to statutory budget reductions in 2013 and totaled approximately $19 billion in fiscal year 2014. However, the program's ability to reach more households is limited by increasing costs in the rental housing market and there remain more eligible low-income households than there are available vouchers. The largest federal program for developing affordable rental housing—the Low Income Housing

Tax Credit (LIHTC) program—cost an estimated $8 billion in forgone revenue in fiscal year 2014. However, other federal support for developing affordable housing—such as HOME Investment Partnerships (HOME)—has decreased and challenges remain for state and local governments to meet increasing demand for affordable rental housing. As a result, the need for affordable rental housing continues to outpace the ability of federal, state, and local governments to supply housing assistance.[3]

We performed our work under the authority of the Comptroller General to conduct evaluations on GAO's initiative to assist Congress with its oversight responsibilities. Our objectives were to (1) identify the federal, state, and local government funded programs in selected jurisdictions that provide rental assistance to low-income households and identify indications of program fragmentation or overlap; (2) assess the extent of intergovernmental collaboration for the provision of rental assistance; and (3) determine what is known about performance at the federal level, at selected state and local jurisdictions, and for the collective performance of the levels of government providing rental assistance.

To conduct this work, we partnered with a group of state and local audit offices.[4] Working as a group, we designed a coordinated audit approach involving multiple audit organizations performing similar audits during roughly the same time.[5] Six of the state and local audit offices—the Washington State Auditor's Office (Washington); the King County Auditor's Office (King County), WA; the Oregon Secretary of State Office, Audits Division (Oregon); City of Portland, Office of the City Auditor, Audit Services Division (Portland), OR; the Multnomah County Auditor's Office (Multnomah County), OR; and Office of the Auditor, City and County of Denver (Denver), CO—conducted these coordinated audits, focused specifically on rental assistance programs for low-income households in their jurisdictions.[6] In addition to reporting on its own programs, Washington also reported low-income rental assistance programs found in the city of Seattle (Seattle), Seattle Housing Authority, and King County Housing Authority. For the purposes of this review, we refer to these six state and local volunteers and Seattle as the "participating audit offices" and the remaining partners as consulting partners. The participating audit offices implemented the audit plan, which included compiling inventories of programs for the respective jurisdiction that address these low-income rental assistance goals, collecting data on key elements of the programs, and identifying performance and collaboration information. We and the participating audit offices worked together throughout our respective audits to answer questions about the audit program and to facilitate information sharing among the partners. We reviewed the results of the participating audit offices' published audit reports and coordinated audit plan results to ensure that the programs reported met the definition for low-income rental assistance and that the information provided matched the questions in the coordinated audit plan and we determined that we could rely on their results. We did not validate the accuracy of the program information reported by the participating audit offices. However, we included questions related to data reliability in the coordinated audit plan implemented by the participating audit offices and we determined that the data were sufficiently reliable for the purposes of this report.

To address the objectives of this report, we analyzed the information the participating audit offices provided as part of their coordinated audit results. Washington, Multnomah County, and Denver also published separate reports.[7] To identify indications of program fragmentation and overlap, we and the participating audit offices analyzed the audit results of the participating audit offices using the definitions from our work on fragmentation and overlap.[8] For example, to identify indications of program overlap we and the participating audit offices analyzed the audit results of the participating audit offices located within the same general geographic area in which the programs were administered to determine whether the reported programs had similar goals or intended beneficiaries, and to determine which agencies, bureaus, or divisions had administrative responsibility for the programs. We also interviewed HUD, U.S. Department of the Treasury (Treasury), and Internal Revenue Service (IRS) officials who participate in the Rental Policy Working Group and reviewed documentation on the agency's rental assistance performance information. For more information on our objectives, scope, and methodology, see appendix I.

We performed our work under authority of the Comptroller General to conduct evaluations on GAO's initiative to assist Congress with its oversight responsibilities. We conducted our work from February 2014 to September 2015 in accordance with generally accepted government auditing standards that are relevant to our objectives. Those standards require that we plan and perform the audit to obtain sufficient and appropriate evidence to meet our stated objectives and to discuss any limitations in our work. We believe that the information and data obtained, and the analysis conducted, provide a reasonable basis for any findings and conclusions based on our audit objectives.

BACKGROUND

Since the 1930s[9], the federal government's role in affordable rental housing has evolved from constructing government owned low-rent public housing to subsidizing rent payments for low-income households and financing the development of affordable housing, including low-income rental housing.[10] Today's federal system for providing these subsidies includes rental assistance programs and federal assistance to state and local governments for affordable rental housing development. The Section 8 rental assistance programs are the largest of HUD's rental assistance programs, and represented in recent years more than a third of HUD's budget, approximately $18 billion. Vouchers, the largest Section 8 rental assistance program, are generally used in the private rental housing market.[11]

Federal assistance to state and local governments for developing affordable rental housing includes broad flexible block grants, special purpose block grants, and programs based in the tax system that can be used for rental, homeownership, or community development purposes.[12] As a result, state and local governments have flexibility and control in using federal resources to fund local housing and community development priorities. For example, HUD's HOME Investment Partnerships program is the largest federal block grant for creating affordable housing for low-income households.[13] The program provides grants to states and local governments to fund a wide range of activities including 1) building, buying, and/or rehabilitating housing for rent or homeownership or 2) providing direct rental assistance to low-income families.

FEDERAL, STATE, AND LOCAL FUNDS ARE USED TO PROVIDE RENTAL ASSISTANCE, BUT FRAGMENTATION AND OVERLAP MAY EXIST ACROSS ALL LEVELS OF GOVERNMENT

Primary Federal Rental Assistance Programs and Assistance to States and Local Governments for Affordable Housing Development

In 2012, we reported that 20 federal government entities administered 160 programs, tax expenditures, and other tools that supported homeownership and rental housing.[14] Based on that housing program inventory, four federal programs represent approximately 92 percent of total obligations and estimated tax revenue losses for low-income rental assistance and affordable housing development programs.[15] These programs included Section 8 rental assistance programs, Public Housing, and two affordable housing development programs—HOME Investment Partnerships Program and LIHTC.

Section 8 Rental Assistance Programs

Section 8 rental assistance includes Housing Choice Vouchers and various project-based rental assistance programs.[16] The Housing Choice Voucher program pays subsidies to landlords so that low-income households can rent private apartments or houses available in the rental market and has provided approximately 2 million vouchers annually to low-income households. In general, households must have very-low incomes—not exceeding 50 percent of the area median income, as determined by HUD. At least 75 percent of new voucher program participants must have extremely-low incomes—not exceeding 30 percent of the area median income. Under the voucher program, an assisted household pays 30 percent of its monthly adjusted income in rent. The remaining portion of the rent is paid through a HUD-subsidized voucher. Public housing agencies (PHAs) can set payment standards (that is, pay subsidies) between 90 percent and 110 percent of the fair market rent for their areas. In order to receive a voucher, a low-income household applies to a local PHA and is placed on a waiting list, unless a household meets special admission requirements.[17] Once a family receives a voucher, it may use the voucher anywhere a voucher program is administered.

Another Section 8 program is project-based rental assistance in which HUD contracts with private property owners to rent housing units to eligible low-income tenants for an income-based rent. No new project-based Section 8 contracts have been awarded since the mid-1980s; however, existing contracts may be renewed and approximately 1 million project-based units remain under contract and receive assistance. In fiscal year 2014, Congress authorized HUD to spend approximately $19 billion for tenant-based rental assistance that includes Housing Choice Vouchers and approximately $9.91 billion for project-based rental assistance. These programs combined to assist more than 3 million households.

Public Housing

HUD subsidizes and regulates low-rent public housing developments that are owned and operated by PHAs. Generally, eligible families living in federally subsidized public housing are low-income; however, 40 percent of available public housing units must be given to extremely low-income families (those with income at or below 30 percent of an area median income). Families living in public housing pay 30 percent of their adjusted income toward rent. PHAs receive several streams of funding from HUD to make up the difference in what tenants pay in rent and what it costs to maintain and modernize public housing. Congress authorized HUD to spend $6.27 billion in fiscal year 2014 and roughly 1 million units are under contract with the federal government. The amount includes $1.87 billion for the Public Housing Capital Fund and $4.4 billion for the Public Housing Operating Fund, which is meant to supplement rents and help meet the operation, maintenance, and capital needs of public housing.

HOME Investment Partnerships Program

The HOME Investment Partnerships Program (HOME) is administered by HUD's Office of Community Planning and Development and is designed to expand the supply of decent, safe, sanitary, and affordable housing. HOME is the largest federal block grant that awards block grants to state and local governments exclusively to create affordable low-income housing. All HOME funds are required to benefit low-income families and at least 90 percent of funds used for rental housing activities or tenant-based rental assistance must benefit families with incomes at or below 60 percent of area median income. Program funding may be used for four purposes: rehabilitation of owner-occupied housing, homebuyer assistance, rental housing construction and rehabilitation, and the provision of tenant-based rental assistance. HOME funds are allocated via formula: 60 percent of program funding is awarded to localities and the remaining 40 percent is awarded to states for areas not served by localities. The HOME formula considers factors related to a participating jurisdiction's supply of substandard, unaffordable, and old rental units, as well as a jurisdiction's population living below the poverty level. HOME grantees must match 25 percent of their HOME grants and submit a plan to HUD detailing their community housing needs and priorities. In fiscal year 2014, the actual obligation for the HOME program was about $1 billion and provided funding to produce approximately 15,000 low-income units. In addition, over 9,500 units received HOME funded rental assistance.

The Low Income Housing Tax Credit

The LIHTC is jointly administered by IRS and state housing finance agencies (HFA). Under this program, tax credits are awarded to developers of qualified projects. State HFAs are responsible for allocating the credit on a competitive basis to owners of qualified low-income rental projects. The tax credits reduce the funds that a developer would otherwise have to borrow. As a result of the lower debt burden, a tax credit property can offer lower, more affordable rents. Provided the property maintains compliance with the program requirements, investors receive a dollar-for-dollar credit against their federal tax liability each year over a period of 10 years. Projects eligible for housing tax credits must meet one of the following two low-income occupancy threshold requirements:

- 20-50 Rule: At least 20 percent of the units must be rent restricted and occupied by households with incomes at or below 50 percent of the area median income (adjusted for household size).
- 40-60 Rule: At least 40 percent of the units must be rent restricted and occupied by households with incomes at or below 60 percent of the area median income (adjusted for household size).

LIHTC is the single largest activity (in terms of foregone revenue) for developing affordable rental housing. The annual cost of LIHTC in foregone revenue is an estimated $8 billion.

Participating Audit Offices Reported Rental Assistance and Development Programs Funded Solely Through Federal, State or Local Dollars, and Also Reported Programs That Used a Combination of Resources

The participating audit offices reported a variety of rental assistance and development programs. The participating audit offices reported that federal, state, and local funds were used to fund the housing programs, as illustrated in figure 1. In some cases, the participating audit offices reported that these funds were combined; in others, only one funding stream was used.

The participating audit offices reported rental assistance programs that were funded solely through federal funds. For example, as shown in table 1 below, participating audit offices reported federal public housing and rental assistance programs including the Housing Choice Voucher programs and other Section 8 programs at housing authorities in King County and Seattle, Multnomah County, Portland, and Denver. The housing authorities of King County, Seattle, and Portland are each designated as Moving to Work sites, a

HUD designation that permits housing authorities to combine federal funding streams into an agency-wide funding pool to allow greater flexibility in operation, and to test innovative approaches for providing housing assistance. In addition, nearly all of the jurisdictions for which programs were reported—except Multnomah County and Portland—used the federal LIHTC program as an incentive for developers of eligible projects to include affordable rental housing.

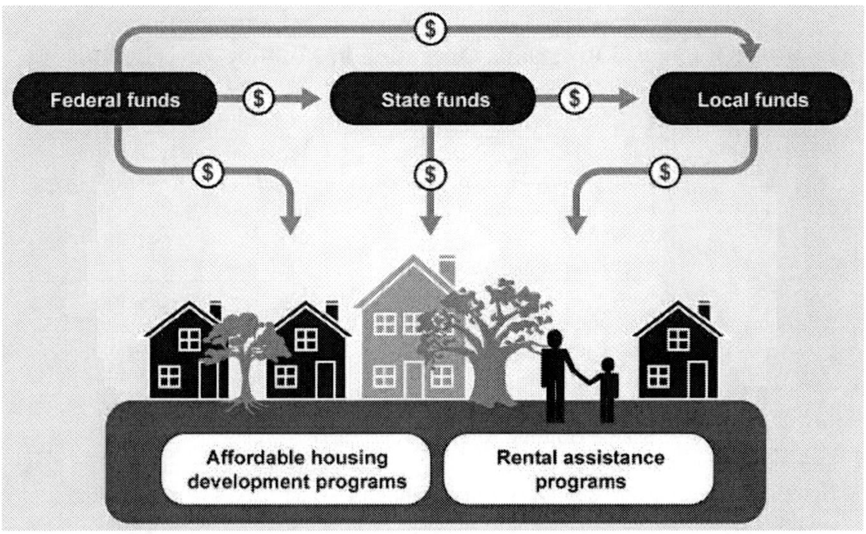

Source: GAO analysis of federal and participating audit offices' program information. | GAO015-645.

Figure 1. Government Funding for Low-Income Rental Assistance and Housing Development Programs.

Participating audit offices in multiple jurisdictions reported HOME Investment Partnerships (HOME) funding as a source of funding used in combination with state or local funding and is not included in this table.

Some of the programs were also funded solely by state or local funds. Two of the Washington State jurisdictions, Washington and Seattle, established dedicated state and local funding sources—a housing trust fund and a housing levy funded by variety of sources including property tax levies—for affordable housing. In addition, programs that provided incentives for affordable housing developers were identified in King County, Seattle, and Portland. For example, inclusionary zoning incentives in Seattle allow developers to build larger facilities than they would be able to otherwise.

Developers in Seattle may receive a residential development bonus that provides additional floor area above a specified base height limit in exchange for including affordable housing in the development. Another type of bonus is also available for additional non-residential floor area in hotel, office, and other developments, in exchange for housing and childcare affordable to low wage workers. Developers may also receive these bonuses by making cash contributions to the City of Seattle for affordable housing development or childcare facilities.

Table 1. Federal Programs Operating in Multiple Jurisdictions

Program	Jurisdiction	Description
Federal Public Housing programs	City and County of Denver King County Housing Authority Multnomah County Portland Seattle Housing Authority	Provides decent and safe rental housing for eligible low-income families,the elderly, and persons with disabilities.
Section 8 Programs	King County Housing Authority City and County of Denver Multnomah County Oregon Portland Seattle Housing Authority	Includes tenant-based voucher and project-based rental assistance programs that provide rental subsidies to low-income families.
Low-Income Housing Tax Credits	Washington King County Housing Authority Seattle Housing Authority Oregon City and County of Denver	Provides federal tax incentives to invest in the development and rehabilitation of affordable rental housing.

Source: GAO analysis of information reported by participating audit offices. | GAO-15-645

Notes: Multnomah County and Portland public housing and Section 8 programs are administered by a quasi-governmental agency called Home Forward. Home Forward is the largest provider of affordable housing in the state of Oregon and oversees approximately 1,980 units of public housing, and approximately 9,390 Section 8 rent assistance vouchers.

Washington State, King County, and Seattle Low-Income Rental Assistance and Housing Development Programs

Washington reported that state resources funded programs for local governments, nonprofits, and community agencies; provided assistance to low-income households at risk of homelessness; and offered financing for affordable housing developers. The Auditor's Office reported that funding sources for Washington state programs included the state's general fund as well as collected recording fees.[18] One of the programs reported by the Auditor's Office was the Housing Trust Fund, which provided capital funding for developing and rehabilitating housing that served low-income households. The trust fund program combined state resources and has awarded nearly $1 billion in funding over the last 25 years to build or maintain nearly 40,000 units of affordable housing. An estimated 70,000 state households are served per year by these units. Table 2 lists the state-level programs reported by Washington for low-income rental assistance and rental housing development that included Washington state funding.

Table 2. Washington State's Low-Income Rental Assistance and Housing Development Programs

Program	Funding source	Description
Housing Trust Fund (HTF)	State	Provides capital funding for the development and rehabilitation of low-income housing.
HTF Operations & Maintenance Fund Program	State	Provides an operating subsidy for HTF projects serving households earning 30% or less of the area median income.
Consolidated Homeless Grant	State	Combines the state's homeless resources into a single grant opportunity for county governments and other designated entities to serve households that are unsheltered, in temporary housing, or at-risk of becoming homeless.
Housing and Essential Needs	State	Provides assistance to eligible residents referred by the Department of Social and Health Services. In addition to rent and utility assistance, the program may cover otheressential needs such as personal hygiene and household cleaning supplies, laundry tokens, bus pass, or gas cards.

Source: GAO analysis of information reported by the Washington Auditor's Office. | GAO-15-645.

King County—Washington's most populous county—reported programs that created and preserved affordable housing and made capital investments to improve low-income communities through relationships with community partners. King County's programs combined federal, state, and local resources to fund grants to local nonprofit organizations, which in turn, provided assistance and services to low-income households at risk of homelessness, as well as providing capital funding to nonprofit developers of low-income housing. In addition, the county offered incentives to private developers to make low-income housing available in market rate projects. For example, King County's Affordable Housing Incentives Program incentivized private housing developers to include affordable units of rental and ownership housing. The incentives program included density bonuses that encouraged developers to build affordable ownership and rental housing in certain areas of King County by allowing developers to build more market rate units than would otherwise be permitted by zoning regulations. In exchange for the bonus market rate units, developers include a specified number of affordable units in the property. The federal sources King County combined with state and local funding included the Emergency Solutions Grants (ESG)[19], Community Development Block Grant (CDBG) and HOME funding.[20] Table 3 lists the low-income rental assistance and rental housing development programs reported by King County that included state or local funding or incentives.

Table 3. King County Low-Income Rental Assistance and Housing Development Programs

Program	Funding Source	Description
Housing Finance Program	Federal Local	Preserves and expands the supply of affordable housing available to low and moderateincome households, including households with special needs.
Affordable Housing Incentives Program	Incentives	Provides incentives, such as density bonuses, to private housing developers to include affordable units of housing within their developments in partnership or in coordination with cities and community stakeholder organizations.
Housing Stability Program	Federal State Local	Provides financial assistance to households for back rent/housing payment and utilities, and provides time-limited counseling to help households overcome a one-time emergency and avoid eviction or foreclosure.

Source: GAO analysis of information reported by the King County Auditor's Office. | GAO-15-645

Note: The King County Affordable Housing Incentives Program is a tool to encourage housing developers to include affordable homes or apartments in their developments and is not a source of funding.

The Washington Auditor's Office reported on Seattle programs that supported rental assistance and affordable rental housing development with federal and local funds. Two of Seattle's programs combined both federal and local resources that provided grants to nonprofit organizations for rental assistance and funding developers of affordable housing. The programs for developers included capital funding, operations and maintenance funding, tax exemptions, and other financial incentives. For example, Seattle's Rental Housing Program combined federal resources with local funding to develop 315 affordable rental apartments and to fund building improvements to preserve 130 affordable rental apartments. The federal resources used by Seattle were HOME and CDBG program funding. The local resources used in Seattle included the Seattle Housing Levy—a dedicated source of funding for affordable housing development.[21] Table 4 lists low-income rental assistance and affordable rental housing development programs for low-income housing developers reported for Seattle that included local funds and incentives.

Table 4. Seattle Low-Income Rental Assistance and Housing Development Programs

Program	Funding source	Description
Rental Housing Program	Federal Local	Funds the development of affordable rental housing.
Multifamily Property Tax Exemption Program	Tax Exemption	Promotes the development of mixed-income buildings by providing owners of multifamily properties with a property tax exemption of up to 12 years on residential improvements in exchange for income- and rent-restricting at least 20% of units.
Incentive Zoning Program	Incentive	Allows developers to obtain more zoning capacity to develop additional units in exchange for making a portion of units available to low- income families. Developers may also makecash contributions to the city for low-income housing in exchange for more zoning capacity.
Operations and Maintenance Fund	Local	Provides a subsidy to housing funded by the Seattle Housing Levy serving those with the highest needs and fewest resources to fill the gap between operating income and expenses.

Table 4. (Continued)

Program	Funding source	Description
Seattle Housing Levy Rental Assistance Program	Local	Provides rental assistance—which is funded through the levy—to low-income families and individuals at risk of homelessness who need help due to a family crisis such as job loss, illness, divorce, or a death in the family.
Homeless Prevention Programs	Federal Local	Provides rental and legal assistance and support services to households at imminent risk of becoming homeless. The program is administered by seven local nonprofit organizations.
Rental Assistance Program	Local	Provides direct assistance on behalf of very low-income households (50% area median income or less) in order to stabilize housing. Assistance may be one time or ongoing and the program is administered by three local nonprofit organizations.
Rapid Re-Housing Program	Local	Provides direct assistance on behalf of very low-income households. Program is administered by five local not-for-profit organizations.

Source: GAO analysis of information reported by the Washington Auditor's Office. | GAO-15-645.

Note: Seattle's incentive program is not a source of funding to private housing developers but rather helps link opportunities for increased development potential with public benefits such as affordable housing. Similarly, the multifamily tax exemption encourages the development of affordable multifamily housing through foregone tax revenue and is also not a source of funding.

Oregon, Multnomah County, and Portland Low-Income Rental Assistance and Affordable Housing Development Programs

Oregon, Multnomah County, and Portland also reported programs that included federal, state, and local resources that provided payments to households, landlords, and utility companies, administrative activities for a public housing program, and financial incentives for the development, acquisition, and rehabilitation of low-income housing. Oregon used federal and state resources to help meet one of its goals to create and preserve opportunities for quality, affordable housing for lower and moderate income

Oregonians. The state allocated federal low-income housing tax credits to encourage the construction and rehabilitation of low-income rental housing and provides funding to community organizations for low-income rental assistance. For example, the state's Low Income Rental Assistance program provided funding to assist low-income households in paying rent and security and utility deposits. This program was administered by community-based agencies that made payments directly to landlords on behalf of 136 very low-income households in 2013.

Multnomah County reported one program—the Short-Term Rental Assistance Program—that combined federal, state, county, and local resources to provide payments to households that were homeless or at risk of becoming homeless. The program was designed to assist residents facing short-term emergencies and at risk of homelessness with rent or mortgage payments, deposits and application fees, move-in costs, and support services. From 2006 through 2010, 6,700 households received an average of nearly 3 months of rental assistance through the program. More recently in 2013, 2,655 households received assistance through nongovernmental community agencies contracted to administer the program. The program consolidated four locally funded short-term housing programs to improve efficiency and results.

Portland combined federal and local resources in its efforts to help Portland residents find a safe, decent, and affordable home to rent or own in a livable neighborhood. To address these goals, Portland used tax increment financing, local tax and permit fees exemptions, and provided financial incentives to housing developers and nonprofits to develop or rehabilitate housing for low-income households. For example, the Housing Investment Program used federal HOME and CDBG funds with local tax increment financing to provide grants and loans to private and nonprofit developers to construct or rehabilitate affordable housing units. From 2011 through 2013, the program provided over $83 million to 36 different development and rehabilitation projects. The projects ranged from remodeling older apartment buildings to constructing new buildings. Nearly all of the projects supported residents at or below 60 percent of median income and many projects also provided support services, such as transitions from homelessness or drug and alcohol treatment. Table 5 shows the state and local low-income rental assistance and rental housing development programs reported by the participating audit offices in Oregon jurisdictions that included state or local funding and incentives.

Table 5. Low-Income Rental Assistance and Housing Development Programs in Oregon Jurisdictions

Jurisdiction	Program	Funding source	Description
Oregon	Low Income Rental Assistance	State Federal	Assists very low-income households by providing rental assistance to those in danger of losing their rental unit because of unpaid rent.
	Elderly Rental Assistance	State Federal	Provides eligible taxpayers with rental assistance from the Department of Revenue.
Multnomah County	Short-Term Rental Assistance Program	Federal State Local	Provides time-limited financial assistance to households that are homeless or at riskof homelessness.
Portland	Housing Investment Program	Federal Local	Provides grants and loans to private and nonprofit developers to construct or rehabilitate affordable housing units.
	System Development Charge Exemption Program	Fee Exemption	Exempts developers from fees that would otherwise be paid to city bureaus during project permitting to promote the development of affordable rental housing.
	Residential Tax Exemption Program	Tax Exemption	Provides ongoing tax exemptions for nonprofit rental housing providers and up to 10-year tax exemptions for new multifamily housing.

Source: GAO analysis of information reported by participating audit offices in Oregon. | GAO-15-645

Note: Portland's fee and tax exemption program are financial incentives measured in foregone revenue and are not sources of funding for developers of affordable housing.

The City and County of Denver Low-Income Rental Development Program

Denver reported one rental housing development program that was not solely funded by federal funds (see table 6). The program combined federal and local resources to address a shortage of affordable rental housing. The

City and County of Denver Audit Office's audit of affordable housing found that the city's largest source of funding was CDBG; however, only a portion of that funding was used for affordable housing.[22] Denver auditors noted that the HOME program is the primary federal source of funding for affordable housing. Denver's Rental Development program combined HOME and CDBG resources with local resources to provide financing for affordable housing developers. In 2014, the program developed or preserved 506 affordable rental housing units. See table 6 for the description of Denver's program that includes local funding and provides financing for developers of affordable rental housing.

Table 6. Denver Low-Income Rental Development Program

Program	Funding source	Description
Rental Development	Federal Local	Provides funding to developers for the acquisition, rehabilitation, or new construction ofrental housing. Other activities within this program include nonprofits applying to adapt existing housing so that it meets Americans with Disabilities Act standards.

Source: GAO analysis of information reported by Denver Audit Services. | GAO-15-645.

Fragmentation and Overlap in Federal Housing Programs and Indications of Fragmentation and Overlap in Programs Reported by Participating Audit Offices May Lead to Inefficiencies

As noted earlier, we found that 20 federal government entities administered 160 programs, tax expenditures, and other tools that supported homeownership and rental housing in fiscal year 2010.[23] We also found instances of fragmentation and overlap throughout these programs.[24] For example, there was overlap in 8 programs and tax expenditures that provided assistance for rental property owners, such as separate project-based rental assistance programs provided by HUD and the United States Department of Agriculture (USDA) Rural Housing Service (RHS) and a program that accelerated depreciation on rental housing administered by IRS.[25] Additionally, there was overlap in the products offered by RHS and HUD (rental assistance and mortgage credit), the functions they perform (portfolio management and preservation), and the geographic areas they serve. We concluded that examining the benefits and costs of housing programs and tax expenditures that address the same or similar areas, and potentially consolidating them, could help mitigate overlap and fragmentation and decrease costs.

Senior HUD Policy Development and Research officials stated that there is fragmentation in developing and providing affordable rental housing because there are several programs that fund the development and provision of housing. Moreover, major affordable housing programs are overseen by three offices within HUD, IRS, and USDA RHS, which can also contribute to fragmentation, overlap, and duplication.[26] The officials also noted that there is fragmentation, overlap, and duplication among some of the rules that govern these programs, which the Rental Policy Working Group has tried to reconcile.

In addition to the fragmentation and overlap we previously found among the federal programs discussed above, we and the participating audit offices also found indications of fragmentation and overlap in the low-income rental assistance and housing development programs that participating audit offices in Oregon and Washington reported in their completed audits. [27] It is important to note that while fragmentation and overlap is often associated with inefficiencies or opportunities for cost savings, we have found that there are instances of positive effects. For example, positive effects may occur where the provisions of benefits, services, or products help meet program goals and objectives.[28]

In the programs reported by participating audit offices in Oregon jurisdictions, we and the participating audit offices found indications of fragmentation among programs that provided financial assistance to households at risk of being homeless, as well as indications of fragmentation and overlap among programs that provided financial incentives to affordable housing developers. First, Oregon and Multnomah County each had a program that included providing financial assistance to households that are at risk of becoming homeless, which may be an indication of fragmentation, as the jurisdictions are involved in the same broad area. Second, three Portland programs provided financial incentives to affordable housing developers—which may be an indication of fragmentation. While these programs included different types of financial incentives to housing developers, they may overlap, as they had similar eligibility for households renting the units. There was fragmentation, overlap, and duplication in rental assistance programs administered by state agencies, according to an Oregon Secretary of State's

Audits Division report.[29] The audits division reported that four state agencies had programs with a mission that focused on rental assistance, which is an indication of fragmentation. Also according to the report, three programs overlapped in providing rent assistance services and two of these programs also showed duplication, as both provided rental assistance to very low-income beneficiaries. In addition, a report by the Office of the Multnomah County Auditor stated that although the depth of services often differs, some of the programs in Multnomah County offered similar types of housing assistance. For example, 15 county programs included rental assistance. The report stated that multiple programs offered similar types of housing assistance, which indicates that there may be some opportunities to streamline services toward greater capacity.[30]

In the programs reported by participating audit offices in Washington jurisdictions, we and the participating audit offices also found that fragmentation and overlap may exist among several of the programs that provided rental assistance to low-income households at risk for homelessness. First, fragmentation may exist among the state, King County, and Seattle rental assistance programs for low-income families at risk of homelessness because each jurisdiction is generally involved in funding these types of programs. Each jurisdiction funded rental assistance programs implemented by local and community-based nonprofit organizations. Second, there may be overlap in each jurisdiction's homeless prevention programs as these programs had similar goals—preventing low-income households from becoming homeless—and targeted similar low-income beneficiaries. Such overlap could impact the efficiency and delivery of services.

Fragmentation and overlap may also exist in programs that provided financial assistance to developers of affordable housing that targeted a similar range of low-income beneficiaries reported by participating audit offices in Washington. Fragmentation may exist because each jurisdiction was generally involved in providing funding for developing affordable rental housing. Such fragmentation could lead to less efficient delivery of affordable rental housing financing. Overlap may also exist because each jurisdiction had programs that provided funding for the development of low-income affordable housing. These programs had similar target beneficiaries and goals which were to develop affordable rental housing for low-income households. This potential overlap could also lead to inefficiencies and ineffective service delivery.

The Rental Policy Working Group and Participating Audit Offices Reported Various Efforts to Collaborate, but Also Reported New Opportunities and Challenges

The Rental Policy Working Group Collaborates with State and Local Governments in Multiple Areas

Inefficiencies as a result of fragmentation, overlap and duplication can result at multiple levels. Our body of work has found that agencies often can realize a range of benefits and savings from addressing issues related to fragmentation, overlap, and duplication, such as improved customer service and decreased administrative burdens and cost.[31] We have also noted that interagency mechanisms or strategies to coordinate programs that address crosscutting issues may reduce potentially fragmented, overlapping and duplicative efforts.[32] As previously discussed, one of the areas we have reviewed and found opportunities to reduce fragmentation and overlap in the area of housing assistance.[33] The federal government plays a major role in ensuring the availability of decent, safe, and affordable rental housing through a variety of single- and multifamily programs that provide rental assistance, public housing, and tax expenditures. Numerous agencies administer fragmented programs, and previous assessments have shown that some programs overlap. For example (as we previously reported), twenty different entities administered 160 programs, tax expenditures, and other tools that supported homeownership and rental housing in fiscal year 2010.[34] Selected rental assistance programs for tenants administered by HUD, Treasury, IRS, and USDA are discussed above.

In order to better coordinate federal rental policy, the Rental Policy Working Group (RPWG) was established in July 2010 by the White House Domestic Policy Council (DPC) and is composed of representatives from DPC, HUD, Treasury, USDA.[35] National Economic Council, and Office of Management and Budget (OMB).[36] The RPWG meets monthly or bimonthly under the auspices of the Domestic Policy Council to discuss its initiatives. The purpose of RPWG is to better align rental requirements across programs and tax expenditures, and thereby increase the effectiveness of federal rental policy and improve participant outcomes. In prior work we found that through interagency collaboration, agencies can improve outcomes and leverage each other's' resources to obtain additional benefits that would otherwise be unavailable.[37] The RPWG does not receive a separate budget, and the agency representatives participate in the group's activities as part of fulfilling their responsibilities at their respective agencies. According to the group's established guiding principles, its efforts have centered on administrative changes that

- responded to the concerns of external stakeholders (rental housing owners, developers, and managers, and state and local housing agency officials);
- required minimal statutory action;
- were realizable at little or no cost or through education, outreach, or the issuance of new guidance or rules; and
- helped create cost and time savings for all parties.

In 2010, the working group solicited recommendations for improved rental policy coordination from external stakeholders, in which administrative changes could increase the effectiveness of federal rental policy and improve participant outcomes, such as overlapping and duplicative administrative property inspection requirements. Within the working group, interagency teams considered the recommendations, reviewed current policies, and identified opportunities for greater federal alignment, increased overall programmatic efficiency, and reduced costs and regulatory burdens. For example, stakeholders noted inefficiencies when a multifamily housing project has multiple layers of assistance (such as subsidies, tax expenditures, or mortgage insurance) from one or more federal agencies. The working group identified 10 initiatives aimed at reducing unnecessary program regulations, lessening administrative barriers so that developers and property owners more easily can participate in programs, reducing duplicative administrative actions to reduce costs for agencies and program participants, and increasing coordination to allow better targeting of agency resources.[38] According to HUD officials, these initiatives are designed to improve states' capacity to preserve affordable rental housing and the "work streams" under the initiatives represent HUD's current efforts to streamline processes and eliminate redundancies.

We have previously concluded that the efforts of the RPWG have been consistent with many key collaborative practices and we have highlighted specific examples of successful collaboration.[39] For example, we highlighted the group's efforts to develop an inventory of federal programs to promote a better understanding of government-wide rental programs and to make decisions about the coordination of related programs across agency lines and between levels of government.[40] However, we have also concluded that the efforts of the group have not taken full advantage of opportunities to reinforce agency accountability for collaborative efforts through the agencies' annual and strategic plans, nor has it expanded its guiding principles to evaluate areas requiring statutory action to generate savings and efficiencies.[41] Methods to build accountability for collaborative efforts include documenting those efforts (and associated goals, strategies, roles and responsibilities, actions or measures to be taken, and timelines) in agencies' annual and strategic plans. We recommended that to further improve HUD, USDA, and Treasury's efforts through the RPWG to consolidate and align certain requirements in multifamily housing programs, the RPWG should take steps to document collaborative efforts in strategic and annual plans to help reinforce agency accountability for these efforts.[42] According to HUD officials, as of July 2015, HUD's strategic planning and annual performance plan and report referenced the RPWG and highlighted its work in improving interagency collaboration in reducing administrative requirements and complexity within and between federal rental housing programs to help achieve the larger goal of delivering more affordable housing at reduced cost.[43]

The RPWG has collaborated with states and localities on four of its initiatives: the Physical Inspections Pilot; Subsidy Layering Review (SLR) Pilot; income reporting and definitions; and market study standards. To achieve more immediate results, the RPWG started with those initiatives that required no statutory action. The physical inspection pilot and SLR pilot were implemented first as the redundancies were "glaringly obvious," according to HUD's most recent progress report.[44] For example, multiple property inspections have been required when funding comes from two or more agencies. The purpose of the pilots is to allow federal, state, local, and private partners to support and test local solutions that lead to program efficiencies.

Physical Inspections

The RPWG launched the physical inspections pilot in six states in November 2011 to test the feasibility of conducting a single, recurring physical inspection for jointly subsidized multifamily housing to satisfy all agencies' inspection requirements.[45] This pilot was designed to eliminate unnecessary physical inspections at rental housing projects subsidized by more than one housing agency, thereby saving scarce local, state, and federal resources while reducing the burden on affordable housing providers and low-income tenants. As we previously reported, USDA, HUD, and Treasury worked with their housing finance agency counterparts at the state level to eliminate duplicative physical inspections of rental housing subsidized through more than one public source.[46] According to a RPWG briefing, participation increased from 6 states to 26 states in 2014 and the pilot avoided 871 duplicative inspections from 2013 to 2014. In 2014, state inspectors were provided with in-person and online training. In 2015, the RPWG is planning to expand the scope to 31 states, perform over 1,000 inspections and provide federal and state agencies the ability to share inspections electronically.[47] According to Treasury and IRS officials they participate in biweekly pilot status meetings with federal, state, and local officials. Treasury and IRS provide federal tax advice for the pilot, such as issuing a notice affirming that HUD (or its agent) could conduct inspections on behalf of the state housing finance agency (or its authorized delegate). In addition, IRS, Treasury, and HUD officials gave presentations that included the physical inspections pilot at state housing association conferences.

Subsidy Layering Review

The RPWG launched the SLR pilot in seven states in 2011 to coordinate the subsidy layering reviews that various federal and state housing program administrators conduct with the aim of eliminating redundancy in the underwriting and review process.[48] Nearly all federal housing programs have statutory requirements requiring the administering agencies to confirm that at the time of making a grant or subsidized loan, the total amount of subsidy being provided by public sources does not exceed eligible costs. According to HUD's most recent progress report, an RPWG survey of participating states found that as of June 2012, two of the six states that responded to the survey had completed SLRs under the alignment MOU, and 24 SLRs had been conducted in those two states.[49] According to this report, most respondents said their offices did not undergo or plan to make any staffing changes, either temporary or permanent, to conduct or review SLRs under the pilot program. Survey respondents reported they are satisfied with the current guidelines established in the SLR-MOU and the level of convenience or perceived convenience in conducting and reviewing SLRs under the SLR-MOU.

Income Reporting and Definitions

The RPWG has also solicited input from states on the income reporting and definitions and market study standards initiatives. Various federal programs that support affordable housing have slightly differing requirements for income certifications and require property managers and owners to submit information on different forms or through different processes, which may lead to inconsistencies in determinations of income and rents or administrative burden. The income reporting and definitions initiative intends to increase education and outreach, to develop a common form for tenant income certification, and to promote single (annual) recertification that would allow owners to coordinate recertifications and satisfy all program requirements at once.

For the income reporting and definitions initiative, according to HUD officials, they solicited input on differing federal affordable housing requirements for income certifications from 10 state housing agency officials, the National Council of State Housing Agencies (NCSHA), and the National Affordable Housing Management Association (NAHMA).[50] NCSHA recommended further discussion of this issue to facilitate better access to income information. NAHMA supports the alignment of varying income definitions, as well as ways to reduce State-to-State variability in compliance requirements. For example, with respect to the LIHTC program, NAHMA members agree that "the absence of cohesive, specific, mandatory Federal guidance means that multi-State developers incur extra costs for, among other items, software and staff training."

Market Study Standards

The market study standards initiative was undertaken in 2010 from stakeholders concerns that there was no national standard of practice for market studies and no broadly acknowledged "keeper" of such standards. The initiative intends to coordinate USDA and HUD guidance on market studies, provide ongoing support and assistance to the National Council of Affordable Housing Market Analysts and other industry advocates, and promote market study literacy among housing and community development practitioners. For the market study standards initiative, according to HUD officials, comments were solicited from state associations. According to a RPWG document, the absence of a fully developed national practice standard and guide for market analyses results in a wide disparity in the content, methodology, quality, and reliability of studies that are used for three primary purposes:

- By State Housing Finance Agencies (HFAs) to allocate Low Income Housing Tax Credits and to establish feasibility for new development of rental housing;

- By HUD-Federal Housing Administration (FHA) and USDA-Rural Development (RD) lenders and field staff to underwrite applications for mortgage insurance or direct loans; and
- By developers, investors, and lenders to identify investment opportunities in rental housing.

Among states, practice varies widely, with some states prescribing methodologies, while others have only loosely defined standards. In spite of existing guidance provided by HUD-FHA and USDA-RD, studies prepared in support of applications for Federal mortgage insurance and direct loan programs are inconsistent in content, methodology, quality, and reliability. According to RPWG documents, the effects of disparate market study practice and quality include confusion, loss of time and extra expense for developers and owners who pay for market studies (that may add little value to the quality of real estate decision making), and higher and/or unforeseen risks of failure, with losses for developers, investors, and lenders.

The initiative intends to coordinate USDA and HUD guidance on market studies, provide ongoing support and assistance to the National Council of Housing Market Analysts (NCHMA)[51] and other industry advocates, and promote market study literacy among housing and community development practitioners. For the market study standards initiative, according to HUD officials, comments were solicited from state associations. These comments were mixed. For example, the NCHMA supports the RPWG assessment that the effects of disparate market study practices and quality can lead to an array of problems, running from confusion to a worst case scenario of financial failure. NCHMA also supports the RPWG's assessment that an independent 'keeper entity' for market study practices standards would be beneficial to the industry. In contrast, the NCSHA does not support the adoption of a national standard of practice of market studies and urged the RPWG to refrain from imposing a "one size fits all" national model as it would not work in all markets.

RPWG's collaboration across federal, state, and local agencies has brought new opportunities to increase efficiencies and program performance. According to HUD officials, progress has been made under the current administration on intra- and interagency collaboration primarily through the RPWG. For example, the RPWG "pushed hard" on coordinating SLR's and helped support state interagency agreements in Minnesota and Ohio. HUD officials also stated that the RPWG has eliminated a number of collaboration challenges at the federal level. For example, it created a venue and mechanism to bring uniformity to different approaches, where possible. HUD and Treasury officials stated that under the current administration, and primarily through the efforts of the RPWG, progress has been made toward improving intra- and interagency collaboration. They also stated HUD's leadership has been very visible in streamlining efforts through the RPWG and has encouraged its field staff to engage with state and local administering agencies on streamlining and efficiency efforts. For example, Treasury officials stated, that there are significant interagency collaboration efforts occurring between Treasury, IRS, HUD, and USDA to develop potential legislative proposals for streamlining LIHTC requirements, and which will be included in Treasury's annual "General Explanations of the Administration's Revenue Proposals" (also known as the "Green Book"). In addition, IRS and Treasury officials stated that RPWG provides state associations with a single federal resource to communicate about low-income housing issues.

Participating Audit Offices Reported Various Efforts to Collaborate with Local, State, and Federal Jurisdictions

All of the participating audit offices reported that they were collaborating with at least one level of government. Oregon, Portland, and Multnomah County all reported collaborating with local governments. For example, Multnomah County officials reported that they had an intergovernmental agreement with other local jurisdictions that outlined each jurisdiction's roles in the Short Term Rental Assistance Program. The leaders of the local jurisdictions met once a month to discuss the program. As part of this arrangement, the jurisdictions shared information on outcomes, investment, management, and risk. For example, each jurisdiction has made a minimum funding commitment to the program and when one of the jurisdictions has trouble meeting this commitment, the group ensures that the funding remains stable through shared investment. Multnomah County officials also reported that this collaboration has resulted in more people served, in maximized resources and in better outcomes. In addition, Oregon also reported collaborating with other state departments to coordinate program eligibility.

Washington and King County reported collaborating with all three levels of government, and Washington reported that Seattle collaborated with the state and local levels. For example, Washington reported that Seattle and the King County Housing Authority centralized their intake and assessment process for families. This enabled families to fill out just one application, which was used by both jurisdictions. The information was stored in a shared database. In another example, Washington collaborated with federal, state, and local governments so that one agency conducted inspections and monitoring activities and wrote a report for each project, which was accepted by all of the funders. As a result, inspection and monitoring activities did not need to be done separately for each funder. In addition, Washington reported that Seattle officials stated that collaboration with other public and private agencies allowed for more resource sharing, innovative strategies, and better leveraging of limited available funding.

Denver reported collaborating with local, state, and federal levels of government. For example, officials reported that the Denver Housing Authority recently developed a 15-member Neighborhood Development Collaborative to lobby for affordable housing initiatives at the state and federal levels. The officials also reported that Denver agencies collaborated with local, state, and federal agencies through a stakeholder group that met quarterly to discuss each jurisdiction's upcoming housing projects to make sure that all participants were aware of the housing activities state-wide and to coordinate where necessary.

Oregon, Multnomah County, Washington, Seattle and Seattle Housing Authority, and King County and the King County Housing Authority also reported barriers to collaboration. These barriers are related to the absence of practices that we previously found can help enhance and sustain collaboration.[52] Oregon, King County, Washington, and Seattle and Seattle Housing Authority reported that incompatible policies, procedures and other means to operate across agency boundaries were barriers. For example, Oregon reported that the Oregon Housing and Community Services department systems did not communicate with other state systems. Hence the client has to navigate the bureaucracy themselves and interact with multiple departments. In addition, Multnomah County, Washington, and the King County Housing Authority reported that a lack of defining and articulating a common outcome or purpose was a barrier. For example, Multnomah County reported that there can be a lack of alignment among the collaborating jurisdictions' priorities and core mission. Defining a common purpose is necessary to overcome significant differences in agency missions, cultures, and established ways of doing business.

HUD, IRS and Participating Audit Offices Reported Varying Levels of Performance Reporting, but There Is Incomplete Information on Collective Performance

HUD, IRS and Participating Audit Offices Reported Varying Levels of Performance Reporting

At the federal level, HUD and IRS reported on the performance of rental assistance programs to varying extents. HUD established a strategic goal to meet the need for quality affordable rental homes in its Strategic Plan 2014-2018.[53] To help it meet this goal, HUD set two strategic objectives. The first of these objectives is to ensure sustainable investments in affordable rental housing. For this objective, in the FY 2013 Annual Performance Report, FY 2015 Annual Performance Plan (performance report), HUD has not established any related performance goals.[54] According to OMB guidance, strategic objectives are tracked through a suite of performance goals. The guidance defines a performance goal to include a performance indicator, a target and a timeframe. In its performance report, HUD identifies fiscal years as timeframes and three performance indicators: the number of households that experience "worst case housing needs," the proportion of very low-income renters facing severe rent burdens, and the percentage of rental units built in the preceding 4 years that had rents below $800. However, HUD did not establish targets for these indicators in fiscal years 2014 and 2015 and states that these indicators are for tracking only. Without related targets, agencies may be unable to demonstrate to key stakeholders, including the Congress, program partners, and the public, that they are tracking progress frequently enough to address any performance issues as they arise. In addition, the performance goals in the annual performance plans provide the Congress with a basis for comparing a program's proposed level of performance against its actual program performance and can help the Congress strengthen government accountability.

The other strategic objective established in HUD's Strategic Plan 2014-2018 is to preserve quality affordable rental housing, where it is needed most, by simplifying and aligning the delivery of rental housing programs. For this objective, HUD has established an agency priority goal of preserving and expanding affordable rental housing programs to serve an additional 121,000 households between October 1, 2013 and September 30, 2015. The performance report lists six performance indicators to track its performance on the agency priority goal: (1) number of families served through HUD rental assistance, (2) number of units converted using the Rental Assistance Demonstration: first component,[55] (3) number of units converted using the Rental Assistance Demonstration: second component,[56] (4) Housing Choice Voucher utilization rate, (5) Public Housing occupancy rate, and (6) Project Based Rental Assistance occupancy rate.

HUD has recently reported on progress toward its strategic objectives and agency priority goal on Performance.gov. For the first strategic objective (to ensure sustainable investments in affordable rental housing), HUD reported that in consultation with OMB, HUD has highlighted this objective as a focus area for improvement. HUD reported that it is pursuing housing finance legislation, which could provide a substantial funding source for the Housing Trust Fund. However, the legislation is not moving forward, which is a significant challenge to HUD in achieving this objective, according to HUD. HUD reported that it is planning to refine the existing metrics to provide a better picture of rental housing availability. In addition, HUD did not report on the performance of the three indicators related to this objective.

Table 7. Agency Priority Goal Indicators, Reported Performance, and Targets for 2014

Indicator	Reported	Target	Met the Target
Number of families served through HUD rental assistance	5,511,132	5,523,223	
Number of units converted using the Rental Assistance Demonstration: First Component	6,167	15,000	
Number of units converted using the Rental Assistance Demonstration: Second Component	7,511	5,161	X
Public Housing Occupancy Rate	96%	96%	X
Housing Choice Voucher budget utilization rate	96.93%	97.56%	

Source: GAO analysis of information on performance.gov. | GAO-15-645.

Note: All of the indicators are reported for fiscal year 2014, except for the Housing Choice Voucher budget utilization rate, which is calendar year.

For the second strategic objective (to preserve quality affordable rental housing by simplifying and aligning the delivery of rental housing programs), HUD reported on Performance.gov that it served an additional 36,128 households, which is 74 percent of its target for the agency priority goal for fiscal year 2014. HUD also reported on the actual performance for five of the six indicators.[57] As shown in table 6 below, HUD reported meeting or exceeding two of the five targets. HUD reported that for the three indicators that HUD did not meets its targets, challenges included an uncertain fiscal environment and slower than expected conversion activity.

However, HUD has not yet published a report on its 2014 performance results consistent with requirements in the GPRA Modernization Act of 2010[58] and OMB guidance which required it to be published in February 2015.[59] According to HUD officials as of June 2015, the 2014 performance report was being reviewed by OMB. Moreover, HUD's performance report for fiscal year 2013 was not published until July 2014; it was required to be published in March 2014, concurrent with the publication of the budget, per OMB guidance. Measuring performance allows organizations to track their progress toward goals and gives managers crucial information on which to base decisions.

We reported in 2012 that information on the overall effectiveness of the CDBG and HOME programs is limited.[60] HUD has faced difficulties in evaluating the impact of the CDBG and HOME block grant programs, because, among other things, such an evaluation would have to compare neighborhoods that received assistance with those that did not. In addition, according to HUD officials and researchers that we spoke with previously, the diversity of activities and lack of statutory targeting requirements makes it difficult to collect information to assess the overall impact of these programs. Our previous work has also identified the difficulties of evaluating the impact of block grant programs that do not have a uniform package of desired outcomes across the country and the common problem of attributing differences in communities' outcomes to the effect of a program without controls for other explanations.

In addition, we previously found that IRS does not set goals or assess performance for LIHTC. [61] We also previously found that data availability was a challenge in assessing tax expenditure performance.[62] IRS collects limited data that it needs to administer and enforce the code and does not use this information to assess the housing production program, such as number and location of LIHTC projects. Although HUD's direct role in the LIHTC program is limited, they have collected project-level information on the program since 1996 because of the importance of LIHTC as a source of funding for affordable housing. We suggested that the Congress consider designating HUD as a joint administrator responsible for oversight of LIHTC.[63] As of September 2015, no action had been taken.

At the jurisdiction level, Washington, King County and the King County Housing Authority, Oregon, and Multnomah County reported having at least one performance goal.[64] For example, one of Oregon's goals included increased housing stability as measured by the percentage of households served who maintain permanent housing for at least 6 months after exiting a program. In addition, one of Multnomah County's goals was that 70 percent of households maintain housing stability at 12 months after the subsidy ends. At the program level within the jurisdictions, most of the rental assistance programs within the jurisdictions had a performance goal and reported on their performance. For example, Washington reported that one of its programs had a performance goal of every eligible person housed and reported that 100 percent of eligible people who requested assistance were housed. King County also reported that one of its program's performance goals was serving 280 new households in new units and reported that 486 households were housed in new units.

Participating Audit Offices Reported Challenges to Assessing Performance

All of the participating audit offices reported challenges to assessing performance. Washington and Portland reported difficulties establishing outcome measures that can be quantified or reported. For example, Portland stated that a challenge was how to quantify and define the social outcome they were trying to achieve. Unlike the homelessness programs, housing retention may not be a good measure or outcome, because the programs want participants to increase their income and move out of subsidized housing, according to Portland. In addition, Seattle, King County Housing Authority, and Multnomah County reported that obtaining data could be difficult. For example, Multnomah County reported that data consistency can be a problem, as its data is gathered by 19 partner agencies.

Washington, Seattle Housing Authority, King County, Oregon, Multnomah County, and Denver also reported that differing policies or performance categories were a challenge. For example, Washington reported that a challenge for the Seattle Housing Authority was that different institutions have differing privacy rules that the Seattle Housing Authority must contend with to gather necessary information. In addition, according to a Multnomah County Auditor Office report, some county programs use output measures such as the number served. The report noted that while these measures are useful for tracking program performance over time, they are not useful for making comparisons of effectiveness across programs. The report recommended a review of performance measures to better understand cost effectiveness and impact of housing assistance programs.[65] The Multnomah County Auditor Office plans to follow-up on the recommendation in December 2015 and a work group has been formed to review data related to housing.

Washington, Seattle, Oregon, Multnomah County, and Denver also suggested steps to enhance outcomes or gain program or process efficiencies. For example, Denver suggested that states and localities should not be required to disperse federal funding too quickly as this can lead to less efficient allocations because of the need to quickly assess conditions and make disbursement decisions. In addition, an Oregon Secretary of State's Audit Division report suggested that inefficiencies could be decreased by establishing compatible policies and procedures and by pursuing collaborative efforts to increase data sharing among programs. The audit division also suggested aligning outcome measures and reporting and eligibility requirements. In addition, the report suggested clearly defining areas of responsibilities and improving evaluations of program effectiveness and efficiencies.66 The audit division plans to follow-up about the status in December 2015.

There Is a Lack of Reporting on the Performance of the Collective Levels of Government

HUD, IRS, and the participating audit offices reported on their performance to varying degrees, and thus there is incomplete information at the federal and participating audit offices' jurisdictions. In addition, HUD, Treasury and IRS officials that are part of the Rental Policy Working Group stated that there is no information on the collective performance of the federal, state, and local jurisdictions that provide rental assistance. Thus it is not known to what extent and how well the local, state and federal rental assistance programs work collectively, for example, to increase the number of households served. Complete and reliable information is a vital component to assessing effectiveness. Federal agencies are required by the Government Performance and Results Act Modernization Act of 2010 (GPRAMA) to describe in their strategic plans and performance plans how they are working together to achieve their goals.[67] GPRAMA's new requirements help drive collaboration and reduce fragmentation. However, the agency-by-agency focus does not provide an integrated perspective of the performance of federal rental assistance programs. GPRAMA further highlights the need for crosscutting[68] performance planning for issues that involve multiple federal agencies and could provide the initial steps toward government-wide performance information. In addition, crosscutting performance measures could be developed through interagency collaboration. Complementary and, where appropriate, common performance measures could permit comparisons of related programs' results and the tools used to achieve those results.

In addition, an OMB policy memorandum that affects federal programs administered by state and local governments, tribes, and territories includes guidance on better results for states, local, and tribal governments. The memorandum states that agencies and their state, local, and tribal partners should review their capacity to generate accurate data to ensure accountability and improve decision making that leads to better outcomes. In addition, the memorandum reported that agencies and their partners should identify opportunities to consolidate and share data across agencies and programs where there are similar reporting requirements.[69]

Compiling and reporting on the collective performance of crosscutting efforts is important in helping to provide a comprehensive picture of how well the different levels of government are providing a service as a whole—in this case, rental assistance. We recognize it is difficult to identify relevant federal, state, and local programs, collect performance information from multiple levels of government, and synthesize the information to reflect the collective performance. However, without information on the government-wide performance of rental assistance, the Congress, decision makers, and stakeholders at all levels of government are hampered in their ability to identify agencies and programs addressing similar missions. They are also hampered in the ability to set priorities, allocate resources, and restructure federal efforts, as needed, to achieve long-term goals. In addition, without such performance information, it is not clear and transparent to the public how governments are collectively providing rental assistance.

HUD has extensive experience with collecting data from state agencies through LIHTC databases that it administers.[70] In addition, HUD is part of the RPWG which has continued to work to implement recommendations that would improve the coordination of government-wide oversight of subsidized rental housing properties. The RPWG has also worked to reduce the administrative burden on affordable housing owners and managers. We have previously reported on practices that help sustain and enhance collaboration among federal agencies.[71] These practices include defining and articulating a common outcome and developing mechanisms to monitor, evaluate, and report results. The RPWG has defined its own priorities and has reported on its progress. HUD, the nation's leading housing agency, in consultation with the RPWG, is well positioned to capitalize on its existing collaboration among federal agencies and with state and local jurisdictions. Thus, working with its state and local partners to develop an approach for compiling and reporting on the collective performance of federal, state, and local rental assistance programs could help pave the way for obtaining data on how well the different levels of government are providing rental assistance as a whole. This effort could start with one or more pilots to test an approach before it is implemented. For example, for one performance indicator, HUD, in consultation with the RPWG, could conduct a pilot to compile and report on the collective performance of relevant federal, state, and local rental assistance programs. One possibility could be to start with one of the rental assistance indicators on which HUD currently reports.

CONCLUSION

The federal government, states, and localities play a significant role in providing rental assistance and developing affordable rental housing for low-income households. Numerous agencies administer these programs, which provide rental assistance, public housing, and tax benefits. In addition, states and localities use federal funds and their own funds to provide rental assistance programs. However, at all levels of government there are indications of program fragmentation or overlap.

HUD has extensive experience with collecting data from state agencies through LIHTC databases it administers. In addition, HUD is part of the Rental Policy Working Group which has taken steps to identify specific areas in which to align sometimes conflicting and redundant requirements. In addition, the Rental Policy Working Group has worked with states and localities on a variety of initiatives to improve states' capacity to preserve affordable rental housing, streamline processes, and eliminate redundancies. Although HUD, IRS and the participating audit offices reported on their performance to varying degrees, one challenge to building upon HUD and the RPWG's successes is that there is incomplete information on the collective performance of the federal, state, and local rental assistance programs. This information would help provide HUD, as the nation's leading housing agency, with important information for assessing and reporting progress on its strategic goal for rental assistance. Complete and reliable information is also a vital component for assessing effectiveness. Although obtaining it is not without challenges however, without information on the government-wide performance of rental assistance, the Congress as well as program managers, other decision makers, and stakeholders at all levels of government are hampered in their ability to identify agencies and programs addressing similar missions. They are also hampered in their ability to set priorities, allocate resources, and restructure efforts, as needed, to achieve long-term goals. In addition, without such performance information, it is not clear and transparent to the public how governments are collectively providing rental assistance.

RECOMMENDATION FOR EXECUTIVE ACTION

To build upon the Department of Housing and Urban Development and the Rental Policy Working Group's efforts to improve coordination of rental assistance, the Secretary of the Department of Housing and Urban Development, in consultation with the Rental Policy Working Group, should work with states and localities to develop an approach for compiling and reporting on the collective performance of federal, state, and local rental assistance programs. Such an effort may begin with one or more pilots to test approaches before they are considered for wider application.

AGENCY COMMENTS AND OUR EVALUATION

We provided a draft of this report to the Secretary of HUD, Commissioner of IRS, and Secretary of the Treasury for review and comment. IRS had no comments on the report. Treasury provided technical comments, which we incorporated into the report.

In its letter, HUD disagreed with the recommendation in our draft report directed to RPWG to work with states and localities to develop an approach for compiling and reporting on the collective performance of federal, state, and local rental assistance programs. HUD stated that the RPWG is not the proper vehicle for this recommendation because the RPWG is an inter-agency collaboration with no dedicated staff or funding. We agreed. Thus, we have revised the recommendation to direct it to HUD, in consultation with the

RPWG, given that HUD is the nation's leading housing agency and is a member of the RPWG and that the RPWG collaborates with different levels of government.

HUD also stated that compiling and reporting collective performance information would require significant funding, staff resources, and information technology efforts. However, our recommendation is to develop an approach for compiling and reporting such data as a first step towards providing information on collective performance. In addition, although we provided one suggestion of how to design an approach by using an existing HUD performance indicator, the recommendation is purposefully not proscriptive, so that HUD, in consultation with the RPWG, can design an approach that is feasible.

HUD stated that the report did not explain what was meant by rental assistance. However, the report defines rental assistance as programs or initiatives with a primary goal of directly or indirectly subsidizing rents for low-income households. In addition, HUD objected to our finding that no information exists on collective performance as being too broadly stated since information already exists on the performance of programs. We agreed. Thus we revised the draft to clarify our point that there is incomplete information on collective performance.

HUD also stated that an analysis of fragmentation or overlap among the federal, state and local programs should include information on federal matching requirements and differentiate between "deep" and "shallow" subsidies. HUD pointed out that Congress enacted matching requirements in order to leverage additional investments and to provide increased local accountability for federal funds and that federal matching requirements should not be considered evidence of unintended fragmentation or overlap. We agree and did not include federal matching requirements in our analysis or consider it to be evidence of fragmentation or overlap. HUD also stated that the report refers to affordable housing without differentiating between programs that are considered to be "deep subsidy" versus "shallow subsidy" programs. HUD stated that a "deep subsidy" program can effectively assist households at the lowest end of the income scale and a "shallow subsidy" program can generally only provide much more modest levels of affordability. HUD noted in an attachment to the letter that the federal government is the primary provider of funding for deep subsidy programs. In this report, our analysis included four federal programs representing 92 percent of total obligations and estimated tax losses for low-income assistance and affordable housing development programs – Section 8 rental assistance, Public Housing, the HOME Investment

Partnerships Program, and the Low Income Housing Tax Credit – that provide varying levels of subsidies and are implemented along with state and local programs. For each of the four federal programs, we included information on income thresholds for eligibility. We also added a footnote on deep and shallow subsidies. Thus, we believe that our report now addressed the difference between deep and shallow subsidies. Moreover, we and the participating audit offices reviewed state and local programs using GAO's definitions of fragmentation and overlap that we developed as noted in the report. In addition, at the federal level, the report refers to previously published work that assessed fragmentation and overlap among federal programs.

HUD also stated that we did not include information on two recent reports on LIHTC—one from GAO and the other the result of a HUD-led effort with assistance from State Housing Finance Agencies.[72] We added information from our LIHTC report, which found that IRS does not set goals or assess performance for LIHTC. The report suggested that Congress should consider designating HUD as a joint administer of LIHTC. We also added information from HUD's LIHTC report by noting that HUD has extensive experience with collecting data from state agencies through the LIHTC databases that it administers.

In addition, in the attachment to HUD's letter, HUD objected to our statement that HUD reported on its performance for only one of its two rental assistance strategic objectives. HUD stated that the worst case housing indicator is valuable as a tracking measure and that a performance measure has not been deemed advisable. However, as we stated in the report, the guidance states that there needs to be a target, which is not included. HUD also stated we ignore several basic issues with measuring housing affordability; however, the report includes HUD's definitions. We also incorporated HUD's technical comments in the report, as appropriate.

Sincerely yours,
J. Christopher Mihm
Managing Director, Strategic Issues

APPENDIX I: OBJECTIVES, SCOPE, AND METHODOLOGY

We partnered with jurisdictions to conduct a pilot effort to develop an approach for examining how federal, state, and local resources might be better coordinated to enhance outcomes and increase intergovernmental efficiency. We performed our work under the authority of the Comptroller General to conduct evaluations on GAO's initiative to assist Congress with its oversight responsibilities. We designed a coordinated audit approach that involves two or more audit organizations performing synchronous audits leading to joint or separate reports. For this pilot effort, we chose to review rental housing assistance for low-income households. Below, we describe how we selected this issue area. Our objectives were to (1) identify the federal, state,, and local government funded programs in selected jurisdictions that provide rental assistance to low-income households and identify indications of program fragmentation and overlap; (2) assess the extent of intergovernmental collaboration for the provision of rental assistance; and (3) determine what is known about performance at the federal level, at selected state and local jurisdictions and for the collective performance of the levels of government providing rental assistance.

We conducted this work in partnership with 25 state and local volunteer audit offices.[1] Six of the state and local volunteers—the Washington State Auditor's Office (Washington); the King County Auditor's Office (King County), WA; the Oregon Secretary of State Office, Audits Division (Oregon), City of Portland, Office of the City Auditor, Audit Services Division (Portland), OR; the Multnomah County Auditor's Office (Multnomah County), OR; and Office of the Auditor, City and County of Denver (Denver), CO—conducted these coordinated audits focused specifically on rental assistance programs for low-income households. In addition, to reporting on its own programs, Washington also reported on the city of Seattle's (Seattle), Seattle Housing Authority and the King County Housing Authority's programs. For the purposes of this review we refer to these six state and local volunteers and Seattle as the participating audit offices and the remaining partners as consulting partners. In addition, the pilot effort led to Washington, Multnomah County, and Denver publishing separate reports.[2] To solicit state and local auditors to participate in this effort, we collaborated with the National Association of State Auditors, Comptrollers, and Treasurers and the Association of Local Government Auditors. The associations' leadership emailed their members a description of the intergovernmental pilot and asked for volunteers to participate.

To identify a policy area for the pilot review, we collaborated with the 25 participating audit offices and contributing partners to identify several potential policy areas using criteria that included

- a mix of programs, funding mechanisms, and levels of government involved;
- the existence of earlier audits on the topic;
- the extent to which coordinated work on the issue would help build a relationship between the audit organizations, as well as the levels of government; and
- the capacity and willingness of each audit organization to work on the topic , which included issues of audit timing, resource commitment, and perceived benefits.

We identified three policy areas as the best fits for the pilot review: workforce training, affordable housing, and local economic development. After conducting background research on the topics and consulting with the state and local volunteers and internal stakeholders, we selected affordable housing because it provided the best match for the criteria listed above. Affordable housing offered a comprehensive array of programs at the federal, state, and local levels that use a variety of funding mechanisms. In addition, there had been previous audits of affordable housing at the federal, state, and local levels.

We narrowed the scope of the pilot to low-income rental assistance programs because affordable housing policy is a broad area and affordable housing programs involve many other issues (such as energy costs and weatherization, food assistance, job training, transportation, home ownership, foreclosure prevention, and neighborhood stabilization) and target various populations (such as the homeless, persons with disabilities, the elderly, veterans, and farm workers). For the purposes of this review, we defined low-income rental assistance to include any programs or initiatives with a primary goal of directly or indirectly subsidizing rents for low-income households. Examples of the federal programs that provide direct subsidies include the Housing Choice Voucher and Public Housing programs and programs that provide indirect subsidies include the Low-income Housing Tax Credit and the Section 202 Supportive Housing for the Elderly programs. Also for purposes of this review, we focused on permanent housing and the federally funded programs that receive the bulk of funding and hence we excluded short-term or temporary programs, temporary shelter programs, and programs targeted at special populations other than the elderly and households with disabilities. Examples of excluded programs include the Tax Credit Assistance Program, the Neighborhood Stabilization Program, Emergency Shelter Grants, and Housing Opportunities for Persons with AIDS.

In collaboration with the participating audit offices and consulting partners, we designed an audit plan for each of the participating audit offices to implement. The audit plan included questions on data reliability for any funding data collected. The audit plan consisted of four components:

1) Identify low-income rental housing assistance performance goals for outputs and outcomes for the respective jurisdiction.
2) Compile inventories of programs for the respective jurisdiction that address these low-income rental assistance output or outcome goals.
3) Collect data on key elements of the programs, such as how the assistance is provided, eligibility for the program, and the program's performance metrics.
4) Examine whether barriers or challenges existed to achieving, establishing, and measuring performance outcomes and measures as well as the extent of intergovernmental collaboration.

The participating audit offices interviewed housing officials in their jurisdictions and submitted the completed audit plans to us. We assisted the participating audit offices in implementing the audit plans by answering questions and facilitating information sharing among the partners. We reviewed the results of the implemented audit plans to ensure that we could rely on their results. For example, we ensured that programs met the definition for low-income rental assistance and that the reported program information matched the questions in the coordinated audit plan. We did not validate or check the accuracy of the information provided by the participating audit offices. However, we included questions related to data reliability in the coordinated audit plan implemented by the participating jurisdictions and determined that the data were sufficiently reliable for the purposes of this report. Because participation in the pilot was voluntary, the coverage varied by state—for Oregon and Washington, we had data from the state, county, and city levels, but for Colorado we only had city and county level data. Further, Washington reported program information for Seattle, the Seattle Housing Authority and the King County Housing Authority.

To describe the programs that provide low-income rental assistance, we used information that the participating audit offices reported on their programs. To identify indications of program fragmentation and overlap, we and the participating audit offices analyzed the audit results reported by the participating audit offices and used definitions from our work on fragmentation and overlap.[3] For example, to identify indications of program overlap we analyzed the audit results of the participating audit offices located within the same general geographic area in which the programs were administered to determine whether the reported programs had similar goals or intended beneficiaries, and which agencies, bureaus, or divisions had administrative responsibility for the programs. Given that Oregon and Washington both had participating audit offices at multiple levels of government and Denver did not, we were unable to assess Denver's programs for fragmentation or overlap. Our work has defined these terms. Fragmentation, in the context of intergovernmental programs, occurs when more than one agency—or more than one organization within an agency—is involved in the same broad area of national need and opportunities exist to improve service delivery. Overlap occurs when there are multiple agencies or programs that have similar goals, engage in similar activities or strategies and activities to achieve those goals, or target similar beneficiaries. GAO's fragmentation, overlap, and duplication evaluation and management guide includes four steps to conducting a fragmentation, overlap, and duplication review.[4] We conducted the first step of identifying indications of fragmentation and overlap, but did not conduct the next three steps, and hence have stated that there are indications of fragmentation and overlap.[5] For example, we did not identify the positive and negative effects of fragmentation and overlap, such as how it can affect program implementation, outcomes, and cost-effectiveness.

To assess the extent of intergovernmental collaboration to provide rental assistance, we analyzed the collaboration information provided by the participating audit offices in the audit results. We also interviewed Housing and Urban Development (HUD), the U.S. Department of Treasury (Treasury), and the Internal Revenue Service (IRS) officials who participate in the Rental Policy Working Group (RPWG) and reviewed documentation on the RPWG's collaboration with states and localities. Based on our most recent housing program inventory published electronically in 2012, HUD and IRS administer five federal programs that represent approximately 92 percent of total obligations and estimated tax revenue losses for low-income rental assistance and affordable housing development programs; thus, we decided to interview HUD, IRS, and Treasury. For our analysis we used our work on collaboration, which describes some of the necessary elements for a collaborative working relationship, such as defining and articulating a common outcome and compatible policies, procedures, and other means to operate across agency boundaries.[6]

To determine what is known about performance at the federal level and at selected state and local jurisdictions, we analyzed the performance information reported by the participating audit offices from the completed audit. We assessed this information using criteria identified in our prior work on performance management which discussed how performance information gives managers crucial information with which to make decisions and influences organizational behavior.[7] We also interviewed HUD, Treasury, and IRS officials who participate in the RPWG about the performance of the combined levels of government and reviewed documentation on the agency's rental assistance performance information.

We performed our work under authority of the Comptroller General to conduct evaluations on GAO's initiative to assist Congress with its oversight responsibilities. We conducted our work on this report from February 2014 to September 2015 in accordance with generally accepted government auditing standards that are relevant to our objectives. Those standards require that we plan and perform the audit to obtain sufficient and appropriate evidence to meet our stated objectives and to discuss any limitations in our work. We believe that the information and data obtained, and the analysis conducted, provide a reasonable basis for any findings and conclusions based on our objectives.

APPENDIX II: STATE AND LOCAL PARTICIPATING AUDIT OFFICES AND CONSULTING PARTNERS

Participating Audit Offices		
States:	Oregon Secretary of State Audits Division	Jeanne P. Atkins Secretary of State Gary Blackmer Director Sheronne Blasi Audit Manager Amanda Lamb Performance Auditor
	Washington State Auditor's Office	Chuck Pfeil, CPA Director of State and Performance Audit Lou Adams, CPA Deputy Director for Performance Audit Nancy Dufoe Principal Performance Auditor Melissa Wade.

Participating Audit Offices		
		CGAP Senior Performance Auditor Tania Y. Fleming Performance Auditor
Counties:	King County, WA Auditor's Office	Kymber Waltmunson County Auditor Ben Thompson Deputy Auditor David Dean Senior Principal Management Auditor
	Office of Multnomah County, OR Auditor	Steve March County Auditor Fran Davison Senior Auditor Marc Rose Performance Auditor
Cities:	Office of the City Auditor (Portland, OR)—Audit Services Division	Mary Hull Caballero City Auditor Drummond Kahn Director of Audit Services Kari E. Guy Senior Management Auditor
	City and County of Denver, CO Office of the Auditor—Audit Services Division	Dennis J. Gallagher Auditor Kip Memmott Director of Audit Services Audrey Donovan Deputy Director Dawn Wiseman Audit Supervisor
Consulting Partners		
States:	California Office of the State Auditor	Elaine M. Howle, CPA State Auditor
	Colorado Office of the State Auditor	Monica Bowers Deputy State Auditor
	Florida Inspectors General	Melinda M. Miguel Chief Inspector General
	Illinois Office of the Auditor General	William G. Holland Auditor General Jim Schlouch Director, Performance Audits
	Mississippi Office of the State Auditor	Sam Atkinson Director, Performance Audit
	Office of the Minnesota State Auditor	Rebecca Otto State Auditor
	Office of the New York State Comptroller	Tina Kim Deputy Comptroller for State Government Accountability

Appendix II. (Continued)

Participating Audit Offices		
	Office of the Auditor of Public Accounts, Commonwealth of Virginia	Jennifer P. Bell Schreck Audit Director, Strategic RiskManagement
Counties:	Mecklenburg County Department of Internal Audit	Joanne Prakapas Director
	Milwaukee County Office of the Comptroller Audit Services Division	Jerome J. Heer Director of Audits
Cities:	City of Austin Office of the City Auditor	Corrie Stokes City Auditor
	City of Dallas Office of the City Auditor	Craig D. Kinton City Auditor
	City of New York Office of the Comptroller	Edward Carey, Jr. Assistant Comptroller, Management Audit
	City of Orlando Office of Audit Services and Management Support	George J. McGowan Director
	City of Phoenix City Auditor Department	Bill Greene City Auditor
Other Governmental Agencies:	The Los Angeles Police Department Internal Audits and Inspection Division	Captain Jodi Wakefield Commanding Officer of AuditDivision
	San Joaquin Hills Transportation Corridor Agencies	Greg Walker Manager, Internal Audit
Associations:	National Association of State Auditors, Comptrollers and Treasurers	R. Kinney Poynter, CPA Executive Director
	Association of Local Government Auditors	Corrie Stokes Past President

End Notes

[1] Bipartisan Policy Center Housing Commission, *Housing America's Future: New Directions for National Policy* (Washington, D.C.: Bipartisan Policy Center, Feb. 2013).

[2] Congressional Research Service, *Department of Housing and Urban Development: FY 2015 Appropriations* (Washington, D.C.: Feb. 11, 2015).

[3] U.S. Department of Housing and Urban Development, Office of Policy and Development Research, *Worst Case Housing Needs 2015 Report to Congress* (Washington, D.C.: April 2015).

[4] See appendix II for a full list of the state and local participating audit offices and consulting partners.

[5] This approach, along with several others, is described by the International Organization of Supreme Audit Institutions (INTOSAI) Working Group on Environmental Auditing. See INTOSAI Working Group on Environmental Auditing, *Cooperation Between Supreme Audit Institutions: Tips and Examples for Cooperative Audits* (November 2007).

[6] For purposes of the report, we defined rental assistance for low-income households to include programs or initiatives with a primary goal of directly or indirectly subsidizing rents for low-income households. (Federal programs that provide direct subsidies include the Housing Choice Voucher and Public Housing programs, for example. Programs that provide indirect subsidies include the Low Income Housing Tax Credit and the Section 202 Supportive Housing for the Elderly programs, for example.) Also for purposes of this report, rental assistance for low-income households excludes short-term or temporary programs (the Tax Credit Assistance Program and the Neighborhood Stabilization Program, for example), temporary shelter programs (Emergency Shelter Grants, for example), and programs targeted at special populations other than elderly and disabled households (Housing Opportunities for Persons with AIDS, for example).

[7] See Washington State Auditor's Office, *Program Understanding Low-Income Housing Rental Assistance Programs*, (Olympia, WA: Aug. 14, 2014), retrieved from http://www.sao.wa.gov/state/Documents/GAO-WA-LIHRA-Data.pdf; Office of the Multnomah County Auditor, *Housing Inventory Special Report fulfilling note from FY-2015 Budget work session* (Portland, OR: Oct. 22, 2014), retrieved from https://multco.us/file/36836/download; and City and County of Denver Office of the Auditor, *Denver Affordable Housing Performance Audit*, (Denver, CO: Nov. 2014), retrieved from http://www.denvergov.org/Portals/741/documents/Audits2014/Denver_ Affordable_Housing _Audit_20Report_11-20-14.pdf.

[8] GAO, *2015 Annual Report: Additional Opportunities to Reduce Fragmentation, Overlap, and Duplication and Achieve Other Financial Benefits,* GAO-15-404SP (Washington, D.C.: Apr. 14, 2015).

[9] United States Housing Act of 1937, Pub. L. No. 75-412, 50 Stat. 888, September 1, 1937

[10] HUD defines the limits of low-income at 80 percent of the median income for the county or metropolitan area. Limits for very-low income and extremely low-income are defined respectively at 50 percent and 30 percent of the area median income. Actual limits may vary from area to area and are available at http://www.huduser.org/portal/datasets.

[11] Under the voucher program, an assisted household pays 30 percent of its monthly adjusted income in rent; the remainder of the rent is paid through a HUD-subsidized "voucher," which generally is equal to the difference between (1) the lesser of the unit's gross rent (generally, rent plus utilities) or a local "payment standard" and (2) the household's payment. "Adjusted income" means the annual income of the members of the family

residing or intending to reside in the dwelling unit, after making a series of mandatory deductions. In the case of public housing, a Public Housing Authority (PHA) may also adopt additional deductions from annual income.

[12] Block grants permit the use of funds for broader categories of activities, such as community development or public health, and give recipients discretion in identifying problems and using grant funds to design programs to address those problems.

[13] In fiscal year 2014, HOME received appropriations totaling $1 billion.

[14] GAO, *Housing Assistance: Opportunities Exist to Increase Collaboration and Consider Consolidation*, GAO-12-554 (Washington, D.C.: Aug. 16, 2012).

[15] In comments on this report, HUD stated that a "deep subsidy" program can effectively assist households at the lowest end of the income scale and a "shallow subsidy" program can generally only provide much more modest levels of affordability.

[16] For example, a project-based voucher program allows public housing agencies (PHAs) to set aside up to 20 percent of their housing assistance for specific housing units if the owner agrees to rehabilitate or construct the units. For more information on federal voucher programs see http://portal.hud.gov/hudportal/HUD?src=/program_offices/public_indian_housing/program s/hcv. 42 U.S.C. § 1437f; 24 C.F.R., Part 982.

[17] GAO, *Housing Choice Vouchers: Options Exist to Increase Program Efficiencies*, GAO-12-300 (Washington, D.C.: Mar. 19, 2012). Special admission requirements are for assistance targeted by HUD, 24 C.F.R. § 982.203.

[18] Washington State's General Fund is the largest pool of funding in the state budget and consists of all major state tax revenues. The General Fund is the principal resource for supporting all state government operations.

[19] The Emergency Solutions Grants program provides funding to (1) engage homeless individuals and families living on the street; (2) improve the number and quality of emergency shelters for homeless individuals and families; (3) help operate these shelters; (4) provide essential services to shelter residents; (5) rapidly re-house homeless individuals and families; and (6) prevent families/individuals from becoming homeless. See the Homeless Emergency Assistance and Rapid Transition to Housing Act of 2009 (the HEARTH Act) enacted as part of Pub. L. No. 111-22, 123 Stat. 1632, 1678 (May 20, 2009).

[20] The Community Development Block Grant (CDBG) program was enacted as part of the Housing and Community Development Act of 1974(Pub. L. No. 93-383, 88 Stat. 633, (Aug. 22, 1974), codified at 42 U.S.C. §§ 5301-5321), and is administered by HUD. The purpose of the CDBG program is to develop viable urban communities by providing decent housing, a suitable living environment, and expanding economic opportunities primarily for low and moderate-income persons. After allocating funds to other activities, the CDBG program distributes 70 percent of the remaining funds through formula grants to entitlement communities—central cities of metropolitan areas, cities with populations of over 50,000, and qualified urban counties—and the remaining 30 percent goes to states for use in non-entitlement communities. 42 U.S.C. § 5301(c).

[21] In November 2009, Seattle voters passed a seven-year, $145 million property tax levy to provide affordable housing opportunities for low-income Seattle residents. The levy has added nearly 2000 affordable rental units and rehabilitated over 400 additional units.

[22] City and County of Denver Office of the Auditor, *Denver Affordable Housing Performance Audit*: (Denver, CO: Nov. 2014.

[23] GAO, *2012 Annual Report: Opportunities to Reduce Duplication, Overlap and Fragmentation, Achieve Savings and Enhance Revenue*, GAO-12-342SP (Washington D.C.: Feb. 28, 2012).

[24] Fragmentation occurs when more than one federal agency—or more than one organization within an agency—is involved in the same broad area of national need and there may be opportunities to improve how the government delivers these services.

[25] Overlap is when there are programs that have similar goals, devise similar strategies and activities to achieve those goals, or target similar users.

[26] Duplication occurs when two or more agencies or programs are engaged in the same activities or provide the same services to the same beneficiaries.

[27] Fragmentation, in the context of intergovernmental programs, occurs when more than one agency—or more than one organization within an agency—is involved in the same broad area and opportunities exist to improve service delivery.

[28] See GAO, Fragmentation, Overlap, and Duplication: An Evaluation and Management Guide GAO-15-49SP (Washington, D.C.: April 14, 2015). The guide highlights the additional steps to evaluate the indications of fragmentation and overlap found in the reported programs. For example, more work would be needed to determine whether there are any benefits or inefficiencies resulting from the existing indications of fragmentation or overlap in the programs reported by the participating audit offices.

[29] Oregon Secretary of State's Audits Division, *Oregon Housing and Community Services Department: Program Duplication, Overlap and Fragmentation*, Report 2013-16 (Salem, OR: July 2013).

[30] Office of the Multnomah County Auditor, *Housing Inventory Special Report (fulfilling note from FY-2015 Budget work session)*, (Portland, OR: Oct. 22, 2014).

[31] GAO, *2015 Annual Report, Additional Opportunities to Reduce Fragmentation, Overlap and Duplication and Achieve Other Financial Benefits*, GAO-15-404SP (Washington D.C.: Apr. 14, 2015).

[32] GAO, *Managing for Results: Key Considerations for Implementing Interagency Collaborative Mechanisms*, GAO-12-1022 (Washington, D.C.: Sept. 27, 2012).

[33] GAO, *2012 Annual Report: Opportunities to Reduce Duplication, Overlap and Fragmentation, Achieve Savings, and Enhance Revenue*, GAO-12-342SP (Washington D.C.: Feb. 28, 2012).

[34] GAO-12-554.

[35] HUD, USDA, and Treasury programs have the shared purpose of financing the development of new rental units or preserving existing units through refinancing or rehabilitation.

[36] Established by Executive Order in 1993, the Domestic Policy Council (DPC) coordinates the domestic policy-making process in the White House, ensures that domestic policy decisions and programs are consistent with the President's stated goals, and monitors implementation of the President's domestic policy agenda. The DPC is chaired by the President and is composed of officials from Executive departments and agencies.

[37] GAO, *Results-Oriented Government: Practices that Can Help Enhance and Sustain Collaboration among Federal Agencies,* GAO-06-15 (Washington, D.C.: Oct. 21, 2005).

[38] The ten initiatives includes: (1) physical inspections,(2) subsidy layering review, (3) income reporting and definitions, (4) market studies standards, (5) financial reporting; (6) common energy efficiency requirements, (7) appraisal primer, (8) capital needs assessment, (9) data sharing on owner defaults, and (10) fair housing compliance enforcement.

[39] We previously identified the following key collaborative practices that can help enhance and sustain collaboration among federal agencies: (1) define and articulate a common outcome; (2) establish mutually reinforcing or joint strategies; (3) identify and address needs by leveraging resources;(4) agree on roles and responsibilities; (5) establish compatible policies; (6) develop mechanisms to monitor, evaluate, and report on results; (7) reinforce

agency accountability for collaborative efforts through agency plans and reports; and (8) reinforce individual accountability for collaborative efforts through performance management systems.

[40] GAO, *Managing For Results: Implementation Approaches Used to Enhance Collaboration in Interagency Groups,* GAO-14-220 (Washington, D.C.: Feb. 14, 2014).

[41] GAO-12-554.

[42] GAO-12-554.

[43] U.S. Department of Housing and Urban Development, *FY 2013 Annual Performance Report, FY 2015 Annual Performance Plan* (Washington: D.C.: July 2014).

[44] RPWG, *Rental Alignment Pilots: Interim Progress Report* (Washington, D.C.: August 2012).

[45] As part of the pilot, state-level teams in Michigan, Minnesota, Ohio, Oregon, Washington, and Wisconsin agreed to merge all required physical inspections into a single inspection protocol with a defined frequency at each multifamily property. The details of this agreement are included in a Memoranda of Understanding (MOU) signed in each state. In addition, the MOUs identify the lead agency for each inspection, determine which pilot properties to inspect, and establish inspection frequency, follow-up, and information-sharing protocols.

[46] GAO-14-220.

[47] The goal of the 2015 Physical Inspections Pilot is to build on the successes of 2014 through the expansion to 31 states and through an increased focus on technology and policy solutions that will create the ability to scale-up in 2016 and sustain alignment. The 31 states are: California, Colorado, Delaware, Georgia, Illinois, Indiana, Kansas, Kentucky, Louisiana, Massachusetts, Michigan, Minnesota, Missouri, Nevada, New Jersey, New Mexico, New York, North Carolina, Ohio, Oregon, Pennsylvania, Rhode Island, South Carolina, Tennessee, Texas, Utah, Virginia, Vermont, Washington, Wisconsin, and West Virginia.

[48] State-level teams in Michigan, Nevada, North Carolina, Ohio, Pennsylvania, South Carolina, and Wisconsin have implemented pilots to align subsidy layering reviews.

[49] RPWG, *Rental Alignment Pilots: Interim Progress Report* (Washington, D.C.: August 2012).

[50] NCSHA represents state housing agencies and its work centers on three federal programs—Housing Bond programs, the Low Income Housing Tax Credit (LIHTC), and the HOME Investment Partnerships (HOME) program. NCSHA is the principal advocate for both Housing Bonds and the LIHTC and is the principal state advocate for HOME. NAHMA advocates on behalf of multifamily property managers and owners whose mission is to provide quality affordable housing. NAHMA's mission is to support legislative and regulatory policy that promotes the development and preservation of decent and safe affordable housing. In addition NAHMA represents 20 regional, state and affordable housing management associations.

[51] The NCHMA, formerly the National Council of Affordable Housing Market Analysts, provides technical guidance and presents opportunities for market analysts and underwriting professionals to discuss current issues, develop professional networks, and gain cutting-edge information with the goal of improving the quality of residential real estate market studies.

[52] GAO-06-15.

[53] U.S. Department of Housing and Urban Development, *Strategic Plan 2014-2018* (Washington D.C: April 2014).

[54] U.S. Department of Housing and Urban Development, *FY 2013 Annual Performance Report, FY 2015 Annual Performance Plan* (July 2014).

[55] The first component of the Rental Assistance Demonstration allows projects funded under the public housing and Section 8 Moderate Rehabilitation programs to convert their assistance to long-term, project-based Section 8 rental assistance contracts.

[56] The second component of the Rental Assistance Demonstration allows owners of projects funded under the Rent Supplement, Rental Assistance Payment, and Mod Rehab programs to convert tenant protection vouchers to project-based vouchers.

[57] The indicator that is not included is the Project Based Rental Assistance occupancy rate, which is the only indicator in the performance plan that does not have a target for fiscal year 2014.

[58] Pub. L No. 111-352, 124 Stat. 3866 (Jan. 4, 2011). The acronym "GPRA" in the act's title refers to the Government Performance and Results Act of 1993. Pub. L. No. 103-62, 107 Stat. 285 (Aug. 3, 1993).

[59] OMB, Circular No. A-11, Preparation, Submission and Execution of the Budget, pt 6, § 260 (August 2012). OMB updated this guidance in its July 2013 and July 2014, and June 2015 revisions to Circular No. A-11.

[60] GAO, *HUD Has Identified Performance Measures for Its Block Grant Programs, but Information on Impact is Limited*, GAO-12-575R (Washington D.C.: May 15, 2012).

[61] GAO, *Low-Income Housing Tax Credit: Joint IRS-HUD Administration Could Help Address Weaknesses in Oversight*, GAO-15-330 (Washington D.C.: July 15, 2015).

[62] GAO, *Opportunities to Reduce Potential Duplication in Government Programs, Save Tax Dollars, and Enhance Revenue*, GAO-11-318SP (Washington, D.C.: Mar. 1, 2011).

[63] GAO-15-330.

[64] A performance goal is a "target level of performance expressed as a tangible, measurable objective- against which actual achievement can be compared including a goal expressed as a quantitative standard, value, or rate." See, GPRAMA, Pub. L No. 111-352, 124 Stat. 3866, 3871 (Jan. 4, 2011).

[65] Office of the Multnomah County Auditor, *Housing Inventory Special Report (fulfilling note from FY-2015 Budget work session)*, (Portland, OR: Oct. 22, 2014).

[66] Oregon Secretary of State's Audits Division, *Oregon Housing and Community Services Department: Program Duplication, Overlap and Fragmentation, Report 2013-16* (Salem, OR: July 2013).

[67] GPRAMA is the statutory framework for performance management in the federal government and updates the Government Performance and Results Act of 1993 (GPRA).

[68] GPRAMA defines crosscutting as "across organizational (such as agency) boundaries". Pub. L No. 111-352, 124 Stat. 3866, 3870 (Jan. 4, 2011).

[69] Office of Management and Budget, *Memorandum for the Heads of Executive Departments and Agencies: Implementing the Presidential Memorandum "Administrative Flexibility, Lower Costs, and Better Results for State, Local, and Tribal Governments"*, MS-11-21 (Washington D.C.: April 29, 2011).

[70] HUD, *Understanding Whom the LIHTC Program Serves: Tenants in LIHTC Units as of December 31, 2012* (December 2014).

[71] GAO, *Results Oriented Government: Practices That Can Help Enhance and Sustain Collaboration among Federal Agencies*, GAO-06-15 (Washington D.C.: Oct. 21, 2005).

[72] GAO, L*ow-Income Housing Tax Credit: Joint IRS-HUD Administration Could Help Address Weaknesses in Oversight, GAO-15-330* (Washington D.C.: July 15, 2015) and HUD, *Understanding Whom the LIHTC Program Serves: Tenants in LIHTC Units as of December 31, 2012* (December 2014).

End Notes for Appendix I

[1] See appendix II for a full list of the state and local participating and consulting partners.

[2] See Washington State Auditor's Office, *Program Understand Low-Income Housing Rental Assistance Programs* (Olympia, WA: Aug. 14, 2014); Office of the Multnomah County Auditor, *Housing Inventory Special Report fulfilling note from FY-2015 Budget work session* (Portland, OR: Oct. 22, 2014); and City and County of Denver Office of the Auditor, *Denver Affordable Housing Performance Audit* (Denver, CO: Nov. 2014).

[3] GAO, *2014 Annual Report: Additional Opportunities to Reduce Fragmentation, Overlap, and Duplication and Achieve Other Financial Benefits,* GAO-14-343SP (Washington, D.C.: Apr. 8, 2014).

[4] GAO, *Fragmentation, Overlap and Duplication: An Evaluation and Management Guide*, GAO-15-49SP (Washington D.C.: Apr. 14, 2015).

[5] The next steps are as follows: 2) identify the potential effects of fragmentation, overlap, and duplication; 3) validate the effects and assess and compare federal programs; and 4) identify options to increase efficiency and reduce or better manage fragmentation, overlap, and duplication.

[6] GAO, *Managing for Results: Implementation Approaches Used to Enhance Collaboration in Interagency Groups,* GAO-14-220 (Washington, D.C.: Feb. 14, 2014) and *Managing for Results: Key Considerations for Implementing Interagency Collaborative Mechanisms,* GAO-12-1022 (Sept. 27, 2012).

[7] GAO, *Managing for Results: Executive Branch Should More Fully Implement the GPRA Modernization Act to Address Pressing Governance Challenges,* GAO-13-518 (Washington, D.C.: June 26, 2013) and *Executive Guide: Effectively Implementing the Government Performance and Results Act,* GAO/GGD-96-118 (Washington, D.C.: June, 1996).

INDEX

E

F

G

H

I

J

L

M

N

O

P

R

S

T

U

V

W

Y